Political Parties in the Reigns of William III and Anne: The Evidence of Division Lists

I. F. BURTON
P. W. J. RILEY
E. ROWLANDS

Bulletin of the
Institute of Historical Research
Special Supplement No. 7
November 1968

POLITICAL PARTIES IN THE REIGNS OF WILLIAM III AND ANNE: THE EVIDENCE OF DIVISION LISTS

Political Parties in the Reigns of William III and Anne: The Evidence of Division Lists

by

I. F. BURTON
P. W. J. RILEY
E. ROWLANDS

UNIVERSITY OF LONDON
THE ATHLONE PRESS
1968

Bulletin of the Institute of Historical Research
Special Supplement No. 7, November 1968

The publication of this Supplement
has been assisted by a generous grant from the
Twenty-Seven Foundation

*Copies of this Supplement may be obtained from booksellers, price £1,
or from the Secretary, Institute of Historical Research,
University of London, Senate House, London* W.C.1

Printed in Great Britain by
SPOTTISWOODE, BALLANTYNE & CO. LTD.
London and Colchester

Foreword

THE lengthy foreword explaining how a work came to be written has mercifully gone out of fashion, but a collaboration of three people is perhaps sufficiently curious to demand an explanation of some kind. Each of us had been involved for some time with work on the reign of William III. Dr. P. W. J. Riley and Edward Rowlands happened both to introduce their discoveries of hitherto unpublished division lists of the house of commons in 1696 to Dr. I. F. Burton who initiated a proposal that the information in them should be brought together and incorporated, with that contained in a third, published but little known list of the same year, to make a single study of the 1696 house of commons. It seemed to all of us that this new information could be dealt with far more significantly in this way than in separate projects, and we therefore agreed to embark on the perils of a three way collaboration. We shared the work of research, interpretation, and exposition and are collectively responsible for what has resulted. It is not for us to say whether we have succeeded, but at least we have emerged still on speaking terms.

Whilst this work was in progress we have been given cause to be grateful to several people. His Grace the Duke of Portland very kindly gave permission for the information from the Council of Trade list to be reproduced in its entirety. Bodley's Librarian supplied photostats of the lists compiled by Samuel Grascombe. Dr. H. Horwitz was good enough to let us have a typescript of his article on the 1698 division list in advance of its publication in the *Journal of British Studies*, November 1966, which would have been too late for us to have made use of it. Finally, P. W. J. Riley wishes to record gratefully that his share in this collaboration was one of the projects made possible by his appointment as a university research fellow by the University of Sheffield from 1962 to 1965.

Contents

REFERENCES

B.I.H.R.	*Bulletin of the Institute of Historical Research.*
Browning, *Danby*	A. Browning, *Thomas Osborne, Earl of Danby.* 3 vols. Glasgow, 1944–51.
Cobbett, *Parl. Hist.*	*Cobbett's Parliamentary History of England.* 36 vols. London, 1806–20.
Commons Journals	*Journals of the House of Commons.*
Eng. Hist. Rev.	*English Historical Review.*
Feiling	Sir Keith Feiling, *A History of the Tory Party, 1660–1714.* Oxford, 1924.
Hist. Jour.	*Historical Journal.*
Horwitz	H. Horwitz, 'Parties, connections and parliamentary politics, 1689–1714: review and revision', *Jour. Brit. Studies*, vi (1966), 45–69.
Jour. Brit. Studies	*Journal of British Studies.*
Kenyon, *Sunderland*	J. P. Kenyon, *Robert Spencer, Earl of Sunderland, 1641–1702.* London, 1958.
Lees	R. M. Lees, 'Parliament and the proposal for a Council of Trade, 1695–6', *Eng. Hist. Rev.*, liv (1939), 38–66.
Somers Tracts	*A Collection of Scarce and Valuable Tracts*, ed. W. Scott. 2nd edn. 13 vols. London, 1809–15.
Vernon	J. Vernon, *Letters Illustrative of the Reign of William III from 1696 to 1708*, ed. G. P. R. James. 3 vols. London, 1841.
Walcott, *English Politics*	R. Walcott, *English Politics in the Early Eighteenth Century.* Oxford, 1956.

Introduction

THE ROLE of political parties in the unreformed House of Commons could be easily detected had the names of members taking part in divisions been officially recorded and much of the controversy concerning the structure of politics under George III can be traced to the absence of such a record. The late Sir Lewis Namier[1] argued that men went into the House of Commons, not as local agents of a central political purpose, but in pursuit of private advantage, sectional interest, social obligation and personal prestige. The influence of this argument has extended to historians and political scientists working in other fields. However, the particular balance existing at the accession of George III between factors such as these and the objectives of a politician which Burke recognised, namely the joining with others of like mind to promote the national interest according to an agreed principle, is not likely to be found at other times since party politics are a necessary and a proper ingredient of representative institutions. In 1760, party counted for less in the balance because the issues which had traditionally divided Whigs from Tories, their attitudes to the Hanoverian succession and protestant Dissent, were dead, but in the reign of Anne, to take an earlier example, these and other issues such as the conduct of the war against Louis XIV were very much alive. There was in existence at that time moreover a highly efficient group of Whig managers—the Junto—dedicated to the pursuit of power by, amongst other methods, the public profession of Whig principles and prepared on no occasion to compromise for any length of time. One would therefore expect to find the balance between what may for convenience be called the personal and the political factors in the total pattern of politics to be very different in 1702 from what it appears to have been in 1760.

This line of argument places us inevitably in the company of those historians who find themselves in conflict with Professor Robert Walcott whose view, advanced at length in his *English Politics in the Early Eighteenth Century*, was that the structure of politics under William and Anne closely resembled that described by Namier.[2] He argued that there were a number of political groups rearranging themselves from time to time in different coalitions according to the exigencies of day-to-day politics. In establishing the existence of these groups he relied heavily, sometimes exclusively, on genealogical evidence to prove family relationship. He made surprisingly little use of such division lists of the period as were available although he himself had been instrumental in drawing attention to the existence of

[1] L. B. Namier, *The Structure of Politics at the Accession of George III* (1929).

[2] R. Walcott, *English Politics in the Early Eighteenth Century* (Oxford, 1956).

twelve such lists.[1] He maintained that although on nine of the issues covered by the lists he had located there was a Whig and a Tory position, in any one of the divisions 'the "Tory" side... includes many who at other times voted "Whig" and vice versa'.[2] Walcott's contention has been undermined by two main developments. First it has become clear that a family relationship is no guarantee of a similar political interest and a detailed examination of some of Walcott's political groups shows them to have had no basis in fact.[3] Secondly there has been the discovery of further lists by J. G. Sperling, G. S. Holmes and W. A. Speck[4] which suggest that the influence of party on voting behaviour under Anne was very strong indeed. The classification of the parliament of 1698 discovered by Henry Horwitz[5] supports the existence of a similar situation in the last years of William III. In addition Horwitz used the 1698 list to undermine Walcott's general thesis by trying to establish something like a consistent voting pattern, but the validity of his argument was reduced by being able to use only one unidentified list as a base and by confining his analysis principally to the divisions of William III's reign. Finally, J. H. Plumb's Ford Lectures,[6] by bringing to light the story of an electoral strife running throughout most of the later Stuart period with a violence such as can only be regarded as the complete antithesis of the torpor which beset politics in the first decade of George III, appear to have demolished the very foundations of Walcott's edifice.

Professor Walcott has since retracted his views as an explanation of the great political issues but still contends that in the ordinary everyday political battles, party counted for very little.[7] The present authors have analysed three division lists not previously examined which together constitute what must be a unique record for the unreformed House of Commons. All three lists were compiled within the space of eleven months so that all the lists deal with virtually the same set of members. These eleven months happen to be the crucial months of 1696 when the late Sir Keith Feiling suggested that a new structure of political allegiances was being established.[8] All three lists of 1696 contain the names of members voting on both sides and one of them deals with nearly every member of this parliament. The lists come

[1] R. Walcott, 'Division lists of the house of commons, 1689–1715', *B.I.H.R.*, xiv (1936), 25–36.

[2] Walcott, *English Politics*, 34.

[3] J. H. Plumb, Review of Walcott, *English Politics*, *Eng. Hist. Rev.*, lxxii (1957), 126–9; H. Horwitz, 'Parties, connections and parliamentary politics, 1689–1714: review and revision', *Jour. Brit. Studies*, vi (1966), 45–69.

[4] J. G. Sperling, 'The division of 25 May 1711, on an amendment to the South Sea Bill: a note on the reality of parties in the age of Anne', *Hist. Jour.*, iv (1961), 191; G. S. Holmes, 'The Commons division on "No Peace Without Spain", 7 December 1711', *B.I.H.R.*, xxxiii (1960), 223; W. A. Speck, 'The choice of a Speaker in 1705', *ibid.*, xxxvii (1964), 21–46.

[5] Horwitz, 45–69.

[6] J. H. Plumb, *The Growth of Political Stability in England, 1675–1725* (1967).

[7] R. Walcott, 'The idea of party', *Jour. Brit. Studies*, i (1961–2), 61.

[8] K. Feiling, *A History of the Tory Party, 1660–1714* (Oxford, 1924), ch. xi.

from quite different sources and were compiled for quite different purposes. Two of them deal, not with fundamental issues of principle which were always likely to arouse Whig and Tory passions, but with ordinary legislation on which, according to Walcott, such passions were likely to remain dormant.

An analysis of these divisions, and a further analysis of the voting records during the period 1689–1714 of the members named in them, demonstrates quite conclusively that the consideration which overwhelmingly determined voting behaviour on all issues during this period was party. Two other important conclusions have also been established: first, that there was a reordering of political forces over the period 1695–6, as Feiling contended, with the result that henceforth ministries became party ministries, or at most, coalitions of one party with a section of another. The polarisation in the Commons had changed from Court and Country to Whig and Tory. The new Tory party described by Feiling appears as a reality, one element in it being a group of former Country Whigs led first by Paul Foley and then by Robert Harley. For its part, the new Whig party had become what for the next seventy years it was essentially to see itself as—the Court party. The second conclusion is that the very substantial accuracy of the division lists of this period can no longer be doubted, a fact which is itself proof that party allegiance was an easily recognisable and well known phenomenon.

No attempt has been made here to write a definitive political history of even the first year of the parliament of 1695–8, but only to introduce what must be looked on as important evidence for such a history, and to present a statistical analysis which it is contended speaks for itself. We begin with a brief account of the parliamentary situation in 1696, then describe in turn each of the three division lists, and finally analyse the evidence from these lists which is set out fully in the form of two appendices.

The Political Situation in the First Session of the Parliament of 1695–8

THE FORMATION of a ministry based on the Whig group later to be known as the Junto had been virtually effected by the spring of 1695.[1] William III's attempt to govern with the support of varying, and sometimes conflicting, groups in parliament, had clearly met with little success. One of the main reasons for this had been the increasing unwillingness of the Montagu-Wharton combination to play second fiddle in a partnership with Nottingham and Carmarthen. This had helped to produce the lack of management and direction which was so much complained of.

The measure of shifting the weight of influence to the Whigs had been steadily urged from 1692 by Sunderland, and, although for a time William chose to ignore his advice, under pressure of circumstances he began from 1693 to move away from the Tories and rely increasingly upon the Whigs: Somers was promoted to Lord Keeper and Trenchard made Secretary of State. In November 1693 Russell was reappointed to the command of the fleet, Nottingham was put out of the ministry, Shrewsbury was made a Secretary and given a dukedom and Montagu became Chancellor of the Exchequer. Godolphin, then a Court Tory, stayed in office but in the teeth of his protests the commissions of customs and excise were changed to make way for Whig supporters. Carmarthen was made Duke of Leeds in an attempt to compensate him for the great reduction in his influence.

It was soon evident that the reconstruction of the ministry did not ensure a majority for the Court in the Commons. After the expulsion of Sir John Trevor in 1695, a new Speaker had to be elected. The Junto's nominee, Sir Thomas Littleton, was defeated by Paul Foley, a Country Whig and notoriously critical of the ministry. The ministry was faced by a forceful opposition composed not only of old style Tories, but also of Country Whigs who looked for leadership to Robert Harley. A move was made to impeach Leeds and the impeachment of Sunderland was probably also being contemplated. William stopped Leeds's impeachment by proroguing parliament and a dissolution followed on 11 October 1695. The subsequent general election constituted an attempt by the new Court managers to obtain a working majority in the Commons, while the opposition, too, had great hopes from a new parliament.

The results of the election seem to have satisfied, initially, both Court and opposition leaders. A great deal of optimism was generated by local victories, and dreams were entertained of massive swings. But, despite the usual talk of 'great struggles' and the 'din' said to have gone on in some

[1] For the events of William III's reign see especially J. P. Kenyon, *Robert Spencer, Earl of Sunderland, 1641–1702* (1958).

constituencies, under the froth there was no dramatic change. The crop of election petitions was no larger than usual and the turnover of members was merely average.[1]

The opening weeks of the new session showed the Junto's optimism to have been misplaced. Paul Foley was re-elected Speaker whilst his most likely opponent, Sir Thomas Littleton, was induced to stay away from the House.[2] A member of the Tory opposition, John Granville, became chairman of the committee on the state of the nation. The opposition was also in a position to challenge, though unsuccessfully, the choice of Littleton as chairman of the committee of supply.[3] In February 1696 the opposition carried its entire list of accounts commissioners by large majorities against the Court's nominees.

In addition, on the two major issues facing parliament at the beginning of this session—the recoinage and the council of trade—the opposition was able skilfully to exploit the parliamentary situation, taking advantage of the surprising disorganisation of the Court. Indeed, it seems hardly too much to say that only the discovery of the assassination plot in February 1696 rescued the Junto ministers, enabling them to establish their control over the Commons by rigorous use of the loyalty issue. Harley himself seems to have taken this view in a letter to John Methuen, written in the summer of 1696:[4]

Upon the meeting of the last Parliament when the necessary forms were despatching... a gentleman took the opportunity and made the first speech was uttered. By the sequel, it seemed to be designed, for he chalked out the lines of the whole proceedings until the plot's discovery interrupted the scheme. Amongst other things a Council of Trade was mentioned as absolutely necessary, and sometime after was voted as one of the heads in the committee upon the state of the nation. When this building was so far erected, the discovery of the plot put everybody's thoughts upon other matters, and left little room to think of receiving trade. Having shewed you that the great struggle of last union was upon this head, you will not wonder a commission is issued out before the meeting of Parliament.

The three lists to be analysed, concerned with the council of trade in January 1696, the price of guineas in March, and the attainder of Sir John Fenwick at the start of the next session in November 1696, support this view of the events of 1696 entirely.

[1] There were just over fifty disputed returns. Over 160 members were new, but more than 130 had served in one or more of the Exclusion parliaments.

[2] John Freke to John Locke, 30 Nov. 1695, Oxford, Bodleian Library, MS. Locke c. 8, f. 201. 'But to the question of the Speaker I must confess to you the Court was so wise to join with their enemies and force their new friends to comply with them by making Sir Thomas Littleton absent at the choice...'.

[3] *Commons Journals*, xi, 343, 30 Nov. 1695.

[4] Robert Harley to [John] Methuen, 30 June 1696, Hist. MSS. Comm., *Portland MSS.*, iii, 577.

A Forecast for the Divisions on the Proposed Council of Trade, 31 January 1695/6

THIS ISSUE of the council of trade was clearly of importance in Harley's mind and, in fact, it provided the opposition with its greatest success in the session of 1695–6. In mercantile circles discontent had become widespread at the general inefficiency of the existing Lords of Trade and the inability of the Admiralty to protect merchant shipping under war conditions. A considerable body of opinion had developed in favour of a new council of trade on which expert membership should predominate over the merely aristocratic.[1] The Court was aware of this dissatisfaction and, because of it, had decided to set up a Board of Trade. By December 1695 a plan had been prepared with the inspiration of John Locke but the delay in putting it into effect[2] opened the way for parliamentary interference in support of the merchants' disquiet.

On 12 December the Court was taken by surprise by a parliamentary move to set up a council of trade. Court managers in the Commons were driven to run to Kensington so that it could be announced at the end of the debate that a council of trade had already been established. This news was received with some scepticism and 'all looked upon it as a trick'. The best the managers could do on this occasion was to obtain an adjournment, carried by only eleven votes after some heated argument.[3] On 2 January 1696, in the committee to consider the state of the nation, the opposition carried by one vote a resolution that the members of the proposed council of trade should be nominated by parliament instead of by the Crown.[4] On 20 January, the Court retaliated by carrying two resolutions which were equally uncongenial to the opposition: that M.P.s should not be eligible for membership of the proposed council, and that members of it should take an oath abjuring James and recognising William as king.[5] As a result, a major confrontation took place when the committee's report was considered in the Commons on 31 January. The opposition, after a period of intensive lobbying, appeared in great strength; in contrast, the Court seems to have been

[1]For the background to this see C. McL. Andrews, *The Colonial Period of American History* (4 vols., New Haven, 1934–8), iv, ch. ix, and R. M. Lees, 'Parliament and the proposal for a Council of Trade, 1695–6', *Eng. Hist. Rev.*, liv (1939), 38–66.

[2]P. Laslett, 'John Locke and the Board of Trade', *William and Mary Quarterly*, 3rd ser., xiv (1957), 370–402.

[3]Monmouth to Locke, 12 Dec. 1695, Bodl. Libr., MS. Locke c. 16, f. 119.

[4]L'Hermitage to the States General, 3/13 Jan. 1695/6, printed Lees, 49–50; dispatch of Frederic Bonnet, 3/13 Jan. 1695/6, *ibid.*, 53–4.

[5]L'Hermitage to the States General, 21/31 Jan. 1695/6, *ibid.*, 50–1.

ill-prepared and ill-organised, a failure blamed by some on the Commons managers, Sir Thomas Littleton and Charles Montagu.[1] The Court was defeated on both counts: M.P.s were voted eligible to serve by 209 to 188, and the oath was dispensed with by 195 to 188.[2] Even though, through the intervention of the assassination plot of February 1696 and the Association which followed it, the Commons' scheme for a council of trade was lost, and the Court's own Board of Trade thus finally won the day, the double defeat of the Court on 31 January was a most significant political event.

No actual division lists have so far come to light, but there is, in the Portland papers, what may very well be the next best thing, namely, a list of about this date which classifies the members of the Commons, and which is almost certainly a forecast in preparation for one or both of these important divisions of 31 January 1696.[3] This document is a list of the members of the Commons in the parliament elected in November 1695. It is made up on four sheets of paper with the addition of an extra sheet for calculations. The sheets, originally separate, have been gummed together down their left-hand edges to form a booklet with the sheet of calculations on top. This calculation sheet originally served as the outer cover, presumably for dispatch by a messenger, and is informally addressed: '10: or 5. door Greys in Lane'. A list of names on a sixth sheet attached to what is now the fifth sheet refers to a later parliament and has nothing to do with the main list. Although the list was found amongst Harley's papers we have found no other evidence connecting it with Harley.

This list, in what is probably a clerk's hand, divides the members into three columns: *Pro*, *D*[oubtful] and *Con*, in the conventional order of constituencies. On each page the columns have been added, the subtotals being transferred to the last sheet and added to give full totals. Some corrections were later made to the list, the subtotals being amended accordingly and transferred to the calculation sheet although the totals on the last sheet remained uncorrected. On the calculation sheet some of the *D*s were reclassified into *Pro* and *Con*, the totals being further amended. On this calculation sheet a computation was also made of a number of absentees, presumably of those whose absence was looked upon as certain.

In all, 504 members are listed with considerable precision, enabling the date of compilation to be fixed with some accuracy, it being clear that nobody was omitted without good cause. Sir John Bucknall (217, Middlesex)[4] and James Sloane (236, Thetford) are in the list, being returned on 8 and 10 January respectively. John Gibson (Portsmouth), returned on 1 February, is not in the list; nor is Thomas Rider (183b, Maidstone), returned on 17 February. Matthew Aylmer is omitted from the list, his election for

[1] Daniel Bret to [Huntingdon], 3 Feb. [16]95[/6], Hist. MSS. Comm., *Hastings MSS.*, ii, 251.

[2] *Commons Journals*, xi, 423. Oddly enough L'Hermitage reverses the figures for the votes. See his letters of 31 Jan. /10 Feb. and 4/14 Feb. 1695/6, printed Lees, 51–2.

[3] British Museum, Loan 29/31, bundle 1.

[4] Numbers following the names of members refer to the list of members in Appendix A: see below, pp. 40–52.

Portsmouth being declared void on 14 January.[1] All this would seem to establish the date of compilation as being somewhere between 14 January and 1 February 1696.

The fact that certain absentees were allowed for indicates that the list was drawn up with some particular occasion in mind rather than as a general state of the House. In this period or thereabouts there were only two issues which involved divisions on the scale envisaged by the compiler: the divisions on the proposed council of trade and the election of the commissioners of accounts for the session. The accounts commissioners were chosen and declared on 4 and 5 February, outside the period, but close enough for the preparation to have been done before 1 February. But the voting for the accounts commissioners was done by written lists[2] so that a straightforward *Pro* and *Con* list of the kind we are dealing with would not have been of much use. The divisions of 31 January on the council of trade seem therefore to have been the most likely occasion for the list.

If this dating is accepted for the list there are three omissions to be explained: John Methuen (418, Devizes), Sir Rowland Gwynn (115, Beeralston) and Thomas Pitt (429, Old Sarum). Methuen was no doubt omitted because he was in Portugal at the time.[3] Gwynn was returned on 10 December 1695 in place of Sir Henry Hobart who had decided to sit for Norfolk which had also returned him. In the list Hobart appears twice—for both Beeralston and Norfolk—so that Gwynn's omission seems to have been a clerical error.[4] Pitt's omission is difficult to account for, although it is possible that he was either in India or in passage.[5]

The list is marked in what may very well be a highly significant fashion, but a careful examination of the marks shows that any attempt to interpret most of them must be so conjectural as to be virtually useless or misleading. These marks are of two main kinds: those done carefully in black ink and those done more crudely in red pencil.[6] Of the black marks, some are reasonably clear in meaning. Various names were crossed out and transferred to other columns in black ink, presumably after further consideration or discussion. These corrections are the ones already referred to which produced the amended subtotals transferred to the calculation sheet. Other names were ticked in black and these correspond almost exactly in number

[1] N. Luttrell, *A Brief Historical Relation of State Affairs from September 1678 to April 1714* (Oxford, 1857), iv, 5.

[2] *Commons Journals*, xi, 428–9.

[3] Browning, *Danby*, iii, 211.

[4] The total number of members on the list, according to the calculation on the list itself, is 505. The duplication of Hobart's name makes the actual number of members listed 504. There were five seats vacant: 74, 312, 328, 422, 482 (see Appendix A). These, with the three missing members and the Speaker make up the total to 513.

[5] When he went out to be Governor he did not arrive in Madras till 6 July 1698: Hist. MSS. Comm., *Fortescue* (*Dropmore*) *MSS.*, i, pp. iv, 2. Nevertheless it is possible that he was visiting India at this time: Sir Tresham Lever, *The House of Pitt* (1947), 3–4.

[6] The distribution of these marks is given in Appendix C: see below, pp. 60–3.

and distribution with the calculation of absentees on the front sheet.[1] But, in addition to these marks, six members are marked with an 'L' in black ink, all but one being Yorkshire members, and thirty-seven members, in the *Pro* and *Con* columns only, are marked with black crosses. Any significance attached to these marks must be entirely conjectural.

Some, and probably all, of the marks in red pencil postdate the black marks, since Arthur Owen (509, Pembrokeshire) has his black tick as an expected absentee cancelled in red pencil. This would seem to indicate that the red pencil marks represent either a last minute revision of categories, or, more probably, an attempt to record, at the time or shortly afterwards, the actual behaviour of members in one or two divisions. The red pencil marks are so scrappily made for the most part that they might well have been done in haste without a firm surface to write on. These red marks are of various kinds. Thirteen names are crossed out in red; some are marked with what appears to be an ampersand or, alternatively, what could be a 'C'; and there is a variety of other red marks, sometimes placed before the name and sometimes after: ticks, check marks sloping forward, check marks sloping backward, dots, and one mark resembling a gibbet. In several instances the marks have been so badly executed that it is difficult to distinguish between ticks, checks and dots. A substantial number of names has more than one mark each. Any interpretation of these marks must be highly speculative, especially since it is very likely that the marking was not complete. There are, for instance, no ampersands (or 'C's) on the last two sheets, and all attempts to reconcile the marks with the division figures of 31 January founder on this omission.

Despite these difficulties, it is possible to offer some tentative conclusions. No one who is known from independent evidence to have voted on that day, or to have spoken on one side or the other and therefore most probably to have voted, is marked with an ampersand (or 'C').[2] This mark may well denote those absent from the division or divisions, in addition to the expected absentees.[3] Furthermore, it is notable that the stalwarts of both sides, the Court Managers, the Court and opposition lists for accounts commissioners, the tellers in the divisions, are unmarked, so that red marks, of whatever kind, seem to denote either some variation in voting pattern from that expected, or, possibly, a confirmation of a voting forecast that was not considered wholly certain. Some support is given to the former view by a comparison of the completely unmarked names with the

[1] There is a discrepancy of one in the *Con* column where there is an extra tick not allowed for in the calculation. This could be explained in a number of ways.

[2] P. Shakerley to Roger Kenyon, 1 Feb. 1695[/6], Hist. MSS. Comm., *Kenyon MSS.*, 398; [Dr. Nathaniel Johnston] to Huntingdon, 4 Feb. 1695[/6], Hist. MSS. Comm., *Hastings MSS.*, ii, 253.

[3] An ampersand could be a useful abbreviation for 'absent'. 'C' would need more explanation. It is odd that one of the *D*[oubtful] members, Craven Howard (421), who was also an expected absentee, should have had his christian name underlined in red. If this was an expression of opinion by whoever marked the list it might explain why absentees could be marked 'C'.

actual numbers in the divisions. The figures for the first division on whether M.P.s could be members of the proposed council would be, including tellers, and using the classification of the list, 211 *Con*, and 190 *Pro*. On the second division, concerning the oath, the figures would be 197 *Con*, *Pro* remaining constant at 190. A count of the completely unmarked members on both sides gives 176 *Con* and 184 *Pro* (counting Sir Henry Hobart once only). It is probable, of course, that the black marks, apart from the black ticks, should be discounted in calculations concerning the divisions. The addition of those marked with either a black cross or a black 'L', or both, but with no red mark would produce *Con* and *Pro* totals of 181 and 193 respectively. The secret of the discrepancies may well lie in the red marks. It is possible that the crossing out in red denotes cross voting, a theory supported by the identity of some, though not all, of those deleted. It may also be that red ticks indicate opposition voting at some stage. Of those who are known to have spoken or voted against the imposition of the oath, four only are marked,[1] each having a red tick before his name.

The temptation to read too much into the evidence of the marks must be resisted, however, and the list considered as simply a forecast, at least until more evidence comes to light which will assist in interpreting the marks. The forecast originally divided the 504 members into 236 *Pro*, 222 *Con* and 46 *D*[oubtful]. Of the 46 *D*[oubtful], 18 were subsequently reclassified into *Pro* and *Con*, producing revised totals of 240 *Pro* and 236 *Con*.[2] Our interest naturally focuses on three groups of members: those whose classification on this single forecast is the opposite of what their later record might give one to expect, those who were left in the category of *D*[oubtful], and those who defected by absence.

Twelve members were classified on the list as *Pro* although their next recorded vote was for the opposition. For six of them the next recorded vote was on Fenwick's attainder and it is likely that the discrepancy was due to their scruples over the attainder rather than a mistaken forecast on the council of trade.[3] The possible exception to this is Sir George Hungerford (401) whose name was crossed out in red which could indicate that in fact he voted for the opposition on the council of trade.

Of the six remaining M.P.s, five were sufficiently Tory to refuse the Association. Two of these, Robert Payne (152) and Thomas Cartwright (240) were marked with red ampersands and were very likely absent. Sir Edward Norreys (268) had been originally classified as *Con*, then changed to *Pro* and finally crossed out in red, a possible indication that he voted for the other side. Henry Holmes (313) was also crossed out in red. It is possible that all four of these members had already defected from the Court by the time the divisions of the council of trade took place. Sir William Morley

[1] Sir Thomas Stanley (188), Thomas Preston (190), Thomas Foley (436) and Edward Harley (439).

[2] Totals corrected on account of Sir Henry Hobart's having been listed twice.

[3] 122 (who appears to have been absent), 281 (for whose attitude on Fenwick see below, pp. 22), 401, 416, 426, 447.

(377) refused the Association and presumably defected on that occasion. John Lewknor's (378) change has no obvious explanation.

A far larger group of thirty-two members were classified as *Con* on the list whose next recorded vote was for the Court. Of these, five only were new members. Two M.P.s, George Oxenden (30) and Hugh Nanney (506), were deleted in red on the list, indicating a possibility that they had voted contrary to the forecast. Two only were marked with red ampersands denoting probable absence. The bulk of these members have a record consistent with being either amongst the number reverting to the Court, probably following the assassination plot of February 1696 after a period of dalliance with the opposition or, alternatively, amongst the supporters of the Duke of Leeds who followed the duke in opposition on the council of trade, in support of the ministry on the price of guineas and again in opposition over Fenwick's attainder.[1] Charles Osborne (449) was Leeds's son and James Herbert (20) his son-in-law, while the three Berties, Peregrine (208), Philip (212) and Charles (213) were his political allies. Among those whose opposition to the Court was hardly likely to survive the assassination plot were Sir Bevill Granville (71), Thomas Erle (135), and Sir Henry Belasyse (253), senior army officers, and Sir Joseph Williamson (181), a placeman and a former Secretary of State under Charles II. Other members to deserve special notice include James Kendall (56) who was promoted to the Admiralty Commission on 4 March 1696, his salary being made payable from the previous Christmas,[2] an appointment which might well have affected his politics. Concerning Nicholas Hedger (311) and Sir Roger Puleston (503) there seems to have been some doubt in the first place. Hedger was originally classified as *Pro* and subsequently changed to *Con* although being unmarked on the list he would seem to have voted that way. Puleston was originally a *D*[oubtful] but changed to *Con.* His name is followed by a red tick. The politics of Sir William Trumbull (266) also seem to have been odd at this time. It seems likely that in these early days of 1696 some members were not at all sure of how they stood. Two such were probably the members for Clitheroe, Christopher Lister and Ambrose Pudsey (196 and 197). Both had been in the previous parliament. The Lancashire Tories expected them to support the opposition in the Commons but in January 1696 they were showing signs of defection. Richard Edge wrote in January to Roger Kenyon: 'You bid me tell you how the Cliderow [*sic*] members go in Parliament; they go with the Liverpoole members perpetually. I think I need say no more than that'.[3] The Liverpool members were both Court men. Nevertheless Lister and Pudsey were classified as opposition on the list and probably voted according to this forecast. Pudsey certainly voted against the imposition of the oath, in spite of having an election petition pending against his return.[4] Later in the year both voted

[1] See below, p. 28. [2] *Calendar of Treasury Books*, x, 1334.

[3] 16 Jan. 1695/6, Hist. MSS. Comm., *Kenyon MSS.*, 395.

[4] Shakerley to Kenyon, 1 Feb. 1695/6, *ibid.*, 398. Richard Edge to Kenyon, 4 Feb. 1695/6, *ibid.*, 399.

for Fenwick's attainder after being omitted from the list on the price of guineas.

Twenty-eight members were left on the list with a classification of *D*[oubtful]. Of these, twelve were new members. Eight members had no other record in 1696 although only two were new members and were presumably poor attenders in the House. Clearly then, there are grounds for supposing that many of the *D*[oubtful] classifications were due to ignorance of how the members stood. Equally clearly there are some instances in which this is not a sufficient explanation, and probably the compiler was aware that some members were sitting on the fence and awaiting developments. Sir Stephen Fox (219) seems to have been habitually discreet.[1] Sir John Fleet (221) was probably behaving with caution on this occasion. Why doubt should have been entertained about Edward Harley (439) is a mystery, although it might indicate that the compiler was not as sure about the political value of family relationships as Professor Walcott allowed himself to be.[2] In the outcome most of the compiler's doubts proved to have been justified. Out of the twenty-eight in this category, ten seem to have been absent (marked with ampersands or black ticks) and eleven others very probably absent (left unmarked in the *D* column).

There was also, in this issue of the council of trade, scope for particular sectional interests to appear. The mercantile community as a whole favoured a council of trade, but the provincial trading interests were afraid that any council nominated by the Crown would be controlled by the London merchants for their own benefit. There are some few signs that the compiler allowed for this as a factor. The two members for King's Lynn were classified as *D*[oubtful] and both seem to have been absent from the divisions. Of the four Durham members, three were classified as *D*[oubtful], and only the fourth, William Lambton (139), who was the only member of the opposition amongst them, classed as *Con*. The three *D*s may all have been absent. One of them, Henry Liddell (141), was a member of a Newcastle coal family. The two Bristol members were under pressure from their constituents to resist London domination and, finally, Robert Yate (290), a Court man and a merchant, was absent.[3] Nevertheless, it should be noted that, strong though these local pressures must have been in some cases, they were either resisted as Yate's colleague at Bristol, Sir Thomas Day (289), seems to have resisted them, or, in the last resort, members chose absence rather than vote against their normal political allegiance. This sort of behaviour seems to have been significantly above average on the council of trade issue in several counties, namely Cheshire, Dorset, Durham, Gloucestershire and Northumberland. In Dorset the conduct of Lord Ashley (120) and Maurice Ashley (126) was the more remarkable in that both were connected with the 'College', a group associated with John

[1] See below, p. 24, where he is noted as having also absented himself from the division on Fenwick's attainder.

[2] Walcott, *English Politics*.

[3] Printed Lees, 57–61.

Locke.[1] Both would have had some knowledge of, and perhaps some concern in, the Court's own Board of Trade scheme. They were classified as *D* and both of them stayed away. It is true, though, that neither of them had a particularly zealous voting record in 1696.[2]

Altogether, it seems that the compiler of the list made mistakes, but that, on the whole, they were surprisingly few. Some of these errors were due possibly to ignorance, or the acceptance of incorrect information at second hand. There were also members who left their intentions deliberately vague, and others who were so cautious that they seldom, if ever, acted upon what political principle they had; but such members were few in number.

The significant points about this forecast are general ones: first, that it was possible to draw up such a list at all so soon after the opening of a new parliament and, secondly, the fact that it provides what is undoubtedly a detailed and well-informed opinion of the extent of the opposition in the Commons which made so much of the running in the first part of the parliamentary session of 1695–6. The strength attributed to the opposition in the list is not mere wishful thinking. The number 236 allocated to the opposition members in the list is very close to the support received by Harley and Foley in the voting for the accounts commissioners—243 votes for Harley and 238 votes for Foley.[3]

[1] See Laslett, *William and Mary Quarterly*, 3rd ser., xiv, 370–402.

[2] Lord Ashley appears only, and rather doubtfully, in the division on the price of guineas: see below, p. 19. Maurice Ashley appears in no other list.

[3] *Commons Journals*, xi, 429.

The List on the Price of Guineas

THIS IS NOT a newly discovered list: it was published in 1696[1] and noticed by E. S. de Beer in 1942,[2] but it escaped Walcott's attention and has not been subjected to analysis. The issue of the recoinage which occupied the Commons' attention at the beginning of the session of 1695–6 equally with the council of trade, was a complex one.

The war with France, begun in 1689, had occasioned a rise in government spending and a vast expansion of government credit. These led, in turn, to inflation at home and to an adverse balance of payments abroad which was increased by the need to make large cash payments overseas to carry on the war.[3] The rate of exchange with Amsterdam deteriorated and the price of silver bullion rose by 25 per cent, from 5*s.* 2*d.* an ounce to 6*s.* 5*d.* This rise affected the domestic coinage in two ways. Since the value of silver coins was fixed by law, good silver money was hoarded, and only clipped and worn money circulated freely.[4] Guineas, on the other hand, although originally intended to pass for 20*s.*, were allowed to find their own level: in 1695 this reached 30*s.*, a premium equivalent to double that enjoyed by silver bullion.[5]

Contemporaries laid the entire blame for this crisis on the bad state of the silver coinage which was merely a symptom of the real disease. As remedies, two schemes were considered by the government.[6] William Lowndes, Secretary of the Treasury, suggested in effect that the pound should be devalued by 20 per cent. He proposed that all coin should be brought in. The good coins, for the most part milled crowns and half-crowns, were to be stamped and re-issued at a value of 6*s.* 3*d.* for a crown. The bad coinage was to be retained and melted down, the owners being reimbursed with new money according to its old face value. This new money would be 20 per cent lighter than the old coins of the same face value. When the crisis had passed, gold guineas would drop to their intended value of twenty-five new shillings. This entire transaction would have involved a loss to the Exchequer of some £1,500,000, representing the difference between the real and face value of about £4,000,000 of clipped coins.

[1] See below, p. 17 and n. 7

[2] E. S. de Beer, 'Division lists of 1688–1715: some addenda', *B.I.H.R.*, xix (1942), 65–6. He wrongly attributes its authorship to Thomas Wagstaffe the elder.

[3] E. V. Morgan, *A History of Money* (1965), 206–7.

[4] Sir John Craig, *The Mint* (1953), ch. xi; C. Jenkinson, 1st Earl of Liverpool, *A Treatise on the Coins of the Realm in a Letter to the King* (1880).

[5] The melting down or export of silver coin was illegal while gold coin was a perfectly legal hedge against inflation. It was, of course, much cheaper to transport gold.

[6] C. R. Fay, 'Lowndes versus Locke', *Cambridge Historical Journal*, iv (1933), 143–55.

The second scheme the government took into its consideration was advocated by John Locke and its essence was deflation. Existing coins were to be accepted at their face value for a limited period and only in payment of taxes and for subscriptions to government loans. After this period, new milled money would be issued at the old standard and clipped coin received only very slightly above its bullion value, the small premium being intended to provide an incentive for recoining. In due course, guineas would be brought down to somewhere between *20s.* and *22s. 6d.*[1]

Locke's plan was supported by Charles Montagu, Chancellor of the Exchequer, John Somers, Lord Keeper, and Sir Isaac Newton. This was the scheme adopted by the government, but the legislation necessary to implement it was pushed through parliament only after a hotly contested struggle which lasted more than three months. The opposition took up the cause of small tradesmen and the people in general who were not in a position to get rid of the clipped coin by payment of taxes, or subscriptions to loans, and who were therefore threatened with serious loss by the government's proposals. It is not easy to trace more than an outline of the parliamentary struggle, but even this indicates that the opposition campaign was expertly led and, from time to time, on the verge of triumph.

As a result of a request in the King's Speech, the Commons considered the state of the coinage in a committee of the whole House. The opposition was able to exploit the rank and file members' ignorance of financial technicalities; they also took advantage of the remarkable disorganisation of the Court. There were complaints from the Court side that government spokesmen were not being seconded in the House despite explicit commands from the king.[2] The Court nevertheless succeeded in securing the passing of eleven resolutions which were adopted by the Commons on 10 December 1695.[3] These resolutions attributed the economic difficulties of the country to the bad state of the coinage. For a remedy they advised the recoinage of the clipped money at the old weight and fineness, the loss to be borne by the public purse. After a date to be fixed, clipped coins were to pass only in payment of taxes and after a further date were not to be legal tender at all. The opposition challenged the principle of a deflationary recoinage but lost by 225 votes to 114.[4] Select committees were appointed on 12 December to prepare a bill on coinage and to draw up an address to the king.[5]

This address requested the issue of a royal proclamation appointing days

[1] While the price of guineas depended in the long run on the state of the market, the government could exercise a powerful, or even decisive, influence upon it by fixing the price at which customs and excise officers would accept them.

[2] Freke to Locke, 30 Nov. 1695, Bodl. Libr., MS. Locke c. 8, f. 201; same to same, 5 Dec. 1695, *ibid.*, f. 204.

[3] *Commons Journals*, xi, 358. This Court success in coinage produced a transference of the opposition's efforts to the council of trade on which they carried their surprise resolution on 12 Dec. 1695: see above, p. 6.

[4] Chandler prints a short account of the debate in *The History and Proceedings of the House of Commons* (1742–4), iii, 5–7.

[5] *Commons Journals*, xi, 359.

when clipped coins were to cease to be legal tender.[1] A proclamation was issued on 19 December.[2] The dates determined on, however, were so close—clipped crowns, shillings and other coins were not to pass except to the Crown after 1 January, 3 February and 2 March respectively, and approximately one month after those dates were not to pass at all—that commerce came virtually to a stop. Thereupon, a further enquiry was instituted by the Commons into the state of the coin from which on 9 January 1696 there resulted much more generous resolutions than those previously voted.[3] All clipped silver money was to be accepted for exchange even though it was of a baser alloy than standard; premiums were offered for handing in unclipped money, and commissioners were appointed to arrange for the exchange of old into new money throughout the country.[4]

Meanwhile, the original bill drawn up on the basis of the resolutions of 10 December, although passing the Commons in spite of delaying tactics by the opposition, ran into trouble in the Lords. The Duke of Leeds proposed an alternative scheme whereby all unmilled coin would be called down to its bullion value at once; persons handing it in would receive, in addition to its bullion value in new milled money, an interest-bearing certificate for an amount equal to the difference between the bullion and the face value of the coin handed in.[5] There were many other Lords' amendments upon which agreement was eventually reached with the Commons, notably one to include worn as well as clipped money within the terms of the bill, but the Leeds proposal was successfully wrecked by the Commons' argument that it was in effect a device for raising supply and therefore not within the Lords' competence.[6]

The government took advantage of the existence of a select committee charged with the task of drawing up a bill in accordance with the Commons resolutions of 9 January, to obtain leave for it to bring in more than one bill. Accordingly, on 14 January, a new bill was introduced into the Commons to remedy the ill state of the coinage.[7] It rapidly passed through all its stages in both houses and received the royal assent on 20 January. By this act,[8] clipped money was to be accepted for payment of taxes up to 4 May, and for subscriptions to government loans up to 24 June, but not otherwise. On the other hand, worn, and even base, money was acceptable so long as it was not virtually mere brass. This measure also met with delaying tactics from the opposition which came very near to success on 15 January when they lost a procedural motion only by 174 votes to 164.[9]

The Court now turned to the second instalment of its deflationary policy,

[1] *Commons Journals*, xi, 363.
[2] *Tudor and Stuart Proclamations*, ed. R. R. Steele (1910), no. 4164.
[3] *Commons Journals*, xi, 384–5.
[4] *Ibid.*
[5] Browning, *Danby*, i, 529–30.
[6] Luttrell, *Brief Historical Relation*, iii, 3.
[7] *Commons Journals*, xi, 385, 390.
[8] 7 and 8 William III c. 1.
[9] *Commons Journals*, xi, 391.

namely its attempt to reduce the price of guineas to a value somewhere between 20*s.* and 22*s.* 6*d.* When the opposition bill to give effect to the resolutions of 9 January was given a second reading on 21 January, a motion was put that the committee receive instructions to consider the price of guineas, but it was lost by 110 votes to 87. Instead, the Court succeeded, on 13 February, in having the price of guineas referred to a special sitting of the committee of the whole House. Nevertheless, the Court failed to have the price of guineas fixed at its figure of 24*s.* The opposition figure of 28*s.* was carried and, on report, approved by the House by 164 votes to 129.[1]

It was at this point that the assassination plot was discovered and from then on the opposition was virtually in continuous retreat, although it regularly contested the ground over which the government advanced. A clause fixing the price of guineas was added to one of the main money bills of the session and, on report, the Court carried an amendment altering the 28*s.* adopted on 13 February to 26*s.* An opposition motion to confirm 28*s.* was lost by 194 votes to 140.[2] Next, the Court removed from the bill giving effect to the resolutions of 9 January all clauses relating to 'the bringing in of milled, broad, or unclipped, Monies, to be exchanged, by Commissioners in the several Parts of this Realm... for their clipped Monies', and confined the measure to 'the encouraging Persons to bring Plate into the Mint, to be coined'.[3] They further proposed the addition of a clause fixing the price of guineas at 22*s.*[4] By 167 votes to 163 the opposition substituted 25*s.* for 22*s.* but the Court then succeeded in having the whole clause rejected by 155 votes to 146.[5] At the third reading on 26 March, the Court had an engrossed clause with a blank for the price of guineas admitted by 173 votes to 129. Next an opposition motion in favour of 24*s.* was lost by 166 to 146. A price of 22*s.* was then accepted without a division. Finally the clause as completed was agreed to by 182 votes to 135.[6]

In the autumn of 1696 a pamphlet appeared entitled *An Account of the Proceedings in the House of Commons in Relation to the Recoining the Clipp'd Money and Falling the Price of Guineas. Together with a Particular List of the Names of the Members consenting and dissenting.*[7] The House of Commons at once took exception to it. A select committee reported on 30 November that according to John Dover, who admitted being the printer, the author was the non-juror, Samuel Grascombe.[8] The arrest of both men was ordered, but Grascombe absconded; he was not arrested until 1698 when it proved impossible to proceed against him since by this time Dover had died

[1] *Ibid.*, 451; see below, p. 18.
[2] *Commons Journals*, xi, 476.
[3] *Ibid.*, 398.
[4] Compare the title of the bill (*ibid.*, 400) with the title of the act (*ibid.*, 533) and its contents (7 and 8 William III c. 19), and see below, p. 18.
[5] *Commons Journals*, xi, 525.
[6] *Ibid.*, 533.
[7] There is a copy in the British Museum and Thomas Wagstaffe junior included a copy in a collection of his father's writings which is now in the Bodleian.
[8] *Commons Journals*, xi, 601.

abroad.[1] Grascombe was admitted to bail and eventually, although the Commons ordered him to be prosecuted in 1699, all proceedings against him lapsed. Grascombe denied being the author of the pamphlet but it seems very likely that he was not speaking the truth.

The pamphlet purports to be a reply to the questions of a provincial correspondent concerning the continued ill condition of the coinage. It asserts, correctly, that gold and silver coin had previously stayed in the country only because they had passed for more than their intrinsic value. Once the government had remedied this situation, by reducing the price of guineas and restoring the weight and fineness of the silver coinage, money again disappeared from circulation. The author's contention is that the proposers of these measures foresaw their outcome as clearly as did their opponents. He admits the responsibility of parliament as the author of the mischief, but contends that those who opposed 'this bill' should be distinguished from those who advanced it. Since the country has no way of knowing which was which, and was ignorant of the history of the affair in parliament, the pamphlet sets out to give, first, 'a short abstract of the progress of this matter in the House of Commons', and secondly 'a list (as far as my memory serves) of all the Yeas and Noes, that is of all the persons who consented and who dissented and who were for and who against the sinking of the guineas etc.'. In fact, only a broad outline of the parliamentary struggle is given which does not go very far to explain the objects of the various pieces of legislation. However, the information is given that commerce was brought to a standstill as a result of the proclamation of 19 December 1695, that the figure of 28*s*. adopted on 13 February 1696 represented a rejection of one of 24*s*. proposed by the government, and that, first by delaying tactics, and then by direct opposition, the Court succeeded in emasculating the bill which was intended to give effect to the resolutions of 9 January.

The author does not state which division his list of members, Yeas and Noes, is intended to refer to, and it is clear that it cannot refer to any particular division at all. There were three divisions, two of them procedural, upon the first abortive coinage bill, one procedural division on the second, and eight concerned with the price of guineas. None of these at all resembles the figures of 204 to 174 given by the lists in the pamphlet. The decisive division on 26 March, which the pamphlet suggests is the one with which the list is concerned, was that against the figure of 24*s*. by 166 votes to 146. The highest vote for the Court was 194 on 28 February and for the opposition 167 on 20 March. It is possible that the pamphlet lists all who supported one side or the other in the eight divisions concerned with the price of guineas; the figures correspond approximately to what would be expected if that were so. However, five of the known tellers in these divisions are not listed by the pamphlet,[2] and it would seem as though the author

[1] Grascombe's own account is in the Bodleian, MS. Rawl. D. 846.

[2] 464 and 443 were both, perhaps surprisingly, Court tellers on 26 March, while 210, 249 and 475 were upon various occasions tellers for the opposition.

had no particular information relating to actual divisions, not even the names of the tellers, but had considerable knowledge of the general attitude of members to this question. Grascombe was an assiduous collector of information and assembler of lists concerning the allegiance of members of the House of Commons, and it is more than likely that he would have been able to compile a list in just such a way.

How accurate is the list? A comparison with the other two lists of 1696 which have now been discovered suggests that it is very accurate indeed. The author of a pamphlet published in 1697, *Reflections upon a Scandalous Libel*,[1] who commented unfavourably upon the patriotism alleged to have inspired the opposition to the Court on the price of guineas, went on to accuse the author of the *Account* of adding the names of some men 'who were either against them, particularly the Lord Ashley and the Lord Henry Cavendish, or out of town, as Mr. William Ashe'. It is notable that only three names are thus challenged, and that of these, Cavendish (90) and Ashe (411) are two of only eight Noes whose inclusion contradicts the evidence of the council of trade list. It has been seen already[2] that for five of the other six there is additional evidence confirming the record of the guineas list. How far this accuracy is a tribute to Grascombe's industry and scholarship, and how far it reflects the fact that the votes of the great majority of M.P.s were easily predictable from their general political position—in other words that their votes were party votes—can be left undetermined for the present.

[1] *Reflections upon a Scandalous Libel entituled An Account of the Proceedings of the House of Commons, in relation to the Re-Coyning the Clipp'd Money, and falling the Price of Guinea's*. There is a copy in the British Museum.

[2] See above, p. 10–11.

The Attainder of Sir John Fenwick

THE WAVE of loyalty produced by the discovery of the assassination plot had made opposition difficult and even dangerous, so that the Court managers, at the beginning of October 1696, were optimistic about the coming session. With the session a week old, Vernon reported to Shrewsbury: 'I don't know that the House of Commons ever acted with greater concert than they do at present. So that I hope this is a very proper time to bring any matter before them one would wish success to'.[1]

Yet the topic which absorbed the House for most of November produced one of the most acrimonious party struggles of the reign. This was the case of Sir John Fenwick who was to provide, on 28 January 1697, the last instance in English history of an execution under a bill of attainder.

Fenwick was a member of an old Northumberland family and had been M.P. for the county. At one time he had served under the Prince of Orange where he is said to have received a severe reprimand for which he never forgave William. As an irreconcilable Tory he had lost all his commissions at the Revolution and he had been forced by other circumstances to sell his estates. On a number of occasions he had been suspected of conspiring against William III and finally he was arrested, on 13 June 1696, for his alleged part in the assassination plot. Threatened with being put on trial for treason, Fenwick promised to make a confession. Court managers hoped that this would implicate members of the opposition in the House, thereby making easier the passage of government business in the forthcoming session. However, those implicated by Fenwick's confession were not opposition Tories but leaders of the administration, notably Shrewsbury, Russell, Godolphin and Marlborough. Devonshire who, as Lord High Steward, had been appointed to manage the affair, handed Fenwick's accusations to the king without informing his colleagues. William appears to have treated Fenwick's allegations with some contumely since he had little cause to doubt the loyalty of the four men, at any rate at that particular time. But the increasing volume of rumour that 'buzzed into people's ears' made it necessary to bring the matter before parliament. The Court hesitated for fear of the effect this step might have on government business, but finally it was decided that Russell should introduce the affair to the House of Commons on 6 November.[2]

On 2 November, the king met Fenwick in a final attempt to persuade him to withdraw his accusations or provide evidence for them; Fenwick refused

[1] Vernon, i, 30.

[2] Kenyon, *Sunderland*, 281–6; Browning, *Danby*, i, 535–7; J. Hodgson and J. H. Hinde, *A History of Northumberland* (7 vols., Newcastle-on-Tyne, 1820–58), iii, 62; A. S. Turberville, *House of Lords under William III* (Oxford, 1913), 99–101.

to do either and so Russell moved in the House that the allegations were 'false and scandalous and a contrivance to undermine the government and create jealousies...'. This resolution was carried without a division, some of the opposition leaders having been taken into the Court's confidence beforehand.

It is not known when the decision was taken to bring in a bill of attainder against Fenwick. The disappearance of one of the two witnesses required under the new Trial of Treasons Act had made impossible Fenwick's conviction in an ordinary court of law. Vernon had mentioned on 3 November the possibility of proceeding by attainder. Sunderland seems to have had no prior knowledge of the decision and opposed the attainder as much as he dared.[1] At least two other members of the administration, Leeds and Devonshire, were later to become bitter opponents of the bill. The opposition was similarly caught unawares. After Russell's first resolution many Tories had drifted away from the House believing the affair to be over; only a small number remained to oppose the introduction of the bill, and they were defeated by 179 to 61. Any hopes the Junto had of securing the co-operation of Harley, Boyle, or other Country members were soon abandoned. Vernon reported to Shrewsbury on the following day:

...I might as well have let them both alone; they were very well in their answers to me, but neither of them shewed any thing of it in the debate. Perhaps they thought it sufficient to be silent. But in the Bill of Attainder, Harley spoke against it, and both of them stayed together at that division. The Speaker, I think, did his part, and was ready to frame fit questions...[2]

From this point onwards the opposition members were better prepared and made full use of the possibilities for delay which were open to them. Boyle, for instance, proposed that a committee should first be set up to decide the question of procedure. Eventually, after a long debate, Fenwick was allowed more time to produce witnesses.[3]

The dubious legality of the bill appears to have caused concern, and not only to opposition members. Vernon described to Shrewsbury the Attorney General, Sir Thomas Trevor's, 'backwardness towards this bill'.[4] Trevor himself expressed his doubts on 13 November:

I am very unwilling to speak any thing in this matter; because, sir, by the place I have the honour to serve his majesty in, as one of his counsel, if it was in the courts below, I must prosecute on behalf of the King: but I am very sensible while I am in this house, I am in another capacity; I am to vote here as a judge, and not as a party.

The debates on 16 and 17 November provided the opposition with the greatest opportunity to proclaim their dislike for the principles of the bill and they divided the House four times on the first day. An attempt to adjourn failed by 163 to 141. Opposition speakers gave up only after a

[1] Kenyon, *Sunderland*, 285–6.
[2] Vernon, i, 48.
[3] The debates are described at length in Cobbett, *Parl. Hist.*, v, 996–1155.
[4] Vernon, i, 59.

further lengthy debate when about forty of their members left the House on account of the late hour. The debate on the following day produced over thirty speeches, some of considerable length. The opposition, led by men of the calibre of Boyle, Finch, Harcourt, Harley, Howe, Temple and Winnington, dominated the discussion. It was argued that the bill subverted the Trial of Treasons Act passed only in the previous parliament, and ran foul of one of the fundamental laws of nature which required two witnesses to prove guilt. Tories reminded the House of the fate of Strafford and Harley recalled the trial of Algernon Sidney. Whilst carefully dissociating themselves from Fenwick's activities, Tories made much of the fact that the bill made members of the House judge and jury of the case. Support also came from two Whigs who were normally Court supporters, Sir Thomas Pelham and Thomas Newport. Both were haunted by the memory of Sidney, who had, according to the former, stood 'upon it as his natural right that they could not proceed against him, there being but one witness...'.[1] In a long speech Newport made clear his own objections to the bill:

Sir, in this matter I look upon myself, as every gentlemen here, to be a judge; and therefore, I will in this case, as in all others, go according to the dictates of my own conscience: I must be saved by my own faith, and never will pin my faith upon another man's sleeve: Perhaps it may be a weakness in my nature, that I am very tender in the matter of blood... It would seem a little strange that the commons of England, that lately were so very careful of the lives of the subject, and were so desirous of passing a bill that did provide that where there were two species of treason in one indictment, and one witness to one species, and another witness to another species, that that should not be good evidence to convict a person of high treason, that they should be attainting a man for treason upon one single evidence! Surely, they will say, we have mightily changed our opinions since last sessions... I hope no man doubts but I am zealous for this government as any man whatsoever; but, let what will come of it, I can't give my vote for passing of this bill.[2]

The bill was nevertheless committed by 182 to 128, to a committee of the whole House, chaired by one of its most violent supporters, Lord Norreys. He reported to the House on 20, and again on 23 November when, after another division, the bill was engrossed 125 to 88. Compared with earlier clashes the final debate on the third reading on 25 November was less impressive. Perhaps, as Vernon suggested, a very loud speech by Mr. Sloane prevented leading speakers on the other side from coming into the debate. Musgrave, Harley and Howe made no contribution. Eventually the bill was passed by 189 to 156, the narrowest majority for the bill during its passage through the Commons. For the next month the bill was heatedly discussed in the Lords where it was finally passed by the slender majority of seven.

The Fenwick affair, and in particular the division of 28 November, has been the subject of considerable speculation by historians. Interest has centred on the effect of the peculiar issues involved which, it has been believed, cut across normal party views. Most comment stems from Vernon's report to Shrewsbury on 26 November:

[1] Cobbett, *Parl. Hist.*, v, 1077. [2] *Ibid.*, 1062–4.

I thought, indeed, it would have passed with a greater majority in the House of Commons, but some had a shyness in a case of life; some could not resist importunities, and some, I must say, sneaked and deserted.[1]

He noted the absence of Secretary Trumbull, Mr. Heveningham, the Vice-chamberlain, Peregrine Bertie, Sir Bevill Granville and the Attorney General; he observed that Sir Thomas Pelham and Sir Richard Onslow voted against the bill. Characteristically Vernon added: 'It may occasion a disgust, if it be thought an indifferent thing, whether men show a firmness to the Government or not, upon so remarkable an occasion'. Later, Macaulay, dealing with the debate, considered that the opposition's arguments had had a telling effect on many moderate Whigs. More recently both Feiling and Ogg have also stressed the effect of the attainder on normal party opinion. Indeed, Ogg asserts that the bill for a while caused disaffection in the House among both Whigs and Tories.[2]

Now, the fortunate discovery of a record of the final division in the Commons on 25 November allows us to test the assumption generally made, that the bill had produced a considerable amount of cross-voting. The list is in a small collection of Fenwick's letters deposited in the British Museum[3] and is evidently a fair copy, having none of the usual markings or emendations to be found on a working list. The author, and the purpose in making the list, are both unknown. The list records, in the conventional order of constituencies, 188 names, including those of the tellers, who supported the bill (three too few), and 161 who were against (three too many). Among the bill's supporters Lord James Russell (109) is counted twice, appearing under both the constituencies for which he had been returned at the general election.[4] Daniel Elliot (72) is counted with those against though curiously marked 'absent', and Peregrine Bertie (208) is recorded as having voted when, according to Vernon, he had abstained.

Hitherto the chief interest has been focussed on the number of Whigs who, for reasons of conscience, opposed the bill. But a comparison with the lists from earlier in the year shows that this number is relatively small. On this evidence, of the 161 listed as voting against the bill, at least 141 were opponents of the ministry. Of the remaining twenty, three, Francis Godolphin (50), Michael Harvey (127) and Sir Marmaduke Wyvill (457) had been listed as *D*[oubtful] on the council of trade list, whilst another, William Cheyne (14b), had not appeared on any previous list. The evidence for the allegiance of three others, Sir George and George Hungerford (401 and 416), and Francis Stonehouse (426), is also inconclusive. They appear

[1] Vernon, i, 82. Vernon may well have overestimated the support for the bill. Many of the divisions were taken at a late hour and, as occurred on 16 November, opposition members tended to leave the House early. An attempt to adjourn the House earlier on 16 November had been defeated by only 21.

[2] T. B. Macaulay, *History of England* (5 vols., 1855), iv, 751–2; Feiling, 324; D. Ogg, *England in the Reign of James II and William III* (Oxford, 1955), 436.

[3] Brit. Mus., Add. MS. 47608.

[4] Tavistock and Whitchurch.

as government supporters on the list concerning the council of trade but were not listed in the coinage pamphlet.[1]

The residue of thirteen is large enough to be significant, though some of the names come as no surprise. Four of them, at least, were Leeds Tories: Philip, Peregrine and Charles Bertie (212, 208, 213), and Charles Fox (423); the Duke of Leeds was extremely angry that the Junto had made a party issue out of the affair.[2] Fox was joint paymaster of the forces in Ireland but was dismissed in 1698. Later, in Anne's reign, he was to attribute his dismissal to his adverse vote on the attainder.[3] His father, Sir Stephen Fox, showed greater discretion by staying away.[4]

The motives of the remaining nine are reasonably clear. Thomas Newport (281), Sir Thomas Pelham (379) and Sir Richard Onslow (357) had expressed their distaste for the bill during the debates. Pelham and Onslow were known as Whigs of some independence of mind. In this vote they ran counter not only to their political friends but to their families as well.[5] Both were again prominent in opposing the standing army in 1698. William Monson[6] probably followed the example of his kinsman, Pelham. William Howard (84), as brother-in-law to Sir John Fenwick, clearly had a pressing reason for opposing the bill. Family influence may also account for the opposition vote of Lord Henry Cavendish (90), son of the Duke of Devonshire. Nathaniel Bond (122), serjeant-at-law, might well have been expressing a lawyer's dislike of proceeding by attainder. The motives of the remaining two, Tobias Jenkins (447) and Robert Monckton (473), are obscure. From the earlier lists they appear to have been firm Court men. However, Jenkins may have been attached to the Leeds group, his family having once been connected with the duke's interest.[7] On the other hand, Monckton[8] had been an ardent supporter of the Revolution. He had retired to Holland in James's reign and had returned with William in 1688. Perhaps disappointment at not having received a place was one of his motives. The Fenwick affair might well have been a crisis in his relations with the Junto, for later he was one of their bitter enemies. The number of consistent Whig supporters who actually voted against the Court on the

[1] Sir George Hungerford (401) was crossed out in red on the council of trade list.

[2] Browning, *Danby*, i, 535–6.

[3] Brit. Mus., Holland House Papers (unbound), Add. MS. 51324.

[4] As he apparently had done on the council of trade: see above, p. 12.

[5] Denzil and Foot Onslow (358 and 366), and Sir John and Henry Pelham (371 and 380), voted for the bill.

[6] Monson (207) was the son of Sir John Monson, of Carleton, Lincs., and Judith, daughter of Sir Thomas Pelham, 2nd Bt. He was later returned at Aldborough on the Pelham interest.

[7] Browning, *Danby*, iii, 142.

[8] Robert Monckton (473) was the eldest son of Sir Philip Monckton, kt., M.P. for Scarborough. He was returned for Pontefract in 1695 and for Aldborough, 1700–13 on Newcastle's interest. He acted as Newcastle's go-between in negotiations with Harley in 1703. See Sir Thomas Lawson Tancred, *Records of a Yorkshire Manor* (1937), 226, 228; Hist. MSS. Comm., *Portland MSS.*, iv, 59, 193.

bill was, therefore, relatively small, though their defection was significant in a House still fairly evenly balanced between Court and opposition. They were, moreover, members of some standing. Vernon's other complaint was that some who should have known better had 'sneaked' away and deserted the Court. In fact, a surprisingly large number of placemen were absent from the division—about twenty in all.[1] In many cases this was probably to be explained simply in terms of absence rather than of abstention. But the absence of the Attorney General (104) and Sir William Trumbull (266), as well as a number of Tory placemen was probably more significant. Sir Thomas Trevor's reservations about the bill of attainder have already been noticed and Trumbull very likely shared them. Trevor wrote to him on 17 January 1697: 'I do not find evidence of any fact against Sir John Fenwick that will amount to more than a great misdemeanour for which he is bailable...'.[2] The absence of Charles Godolphin (51), Edward and George Nicholas (132 and 252), Ranelagh (373), Sir Henry Goodricke (461), Sir Stephen Fox (219) and possibly Francis Robarts (64) seems to show that other Court Tories besides the Leeds group recognised the Fenwick affair as essentially a party issue.

Finally, there remain those Tories who, according to Ogg, feared the possible consequences of a true Fenwick confession and voted for his execution, to be rid of a man who might have implicated them. Fourteen members[3] who can be classified from the earlier lists as opposition members supported the bill—not a surprisingly large number. Few, if any, represent quasi-Jacobites quaking in the shadow of the block, although perhaps the two Clitheroe members were choosing discretion in dissociating themselves from the more extreme elements in their county.[4] Others belong to the flow of members away from the opposition after the discovery of the assassination plot, sometimes under the added stimulus of a place, or the prospect of a place, at Court. William Farrer was, perhaps, hoping for employment.[5] Constituency pressure may well have influenced Samuel Fuller and George England, the two members for Great Yarmouth.[6] Two members—Sir William Ellis (215) and Thomas Foley, might, as distinguished Country

[1] 7, 24, 51, 60, 64, 104, 132, 180, 219–20, 237, 246, 252, 266, 305, 361, 373, 449, 461, 489. In addition four army officers were absent: 12, 15, 61, 71.

[2] Hist. MSS. Comm., *Downshire MSS.*, i, 613.

[3] 3, 101, 138, 150, 196–7, 215, 233–4, 359, 436, 454–5, 496.

[4] Ambrose Pudsey and Christopher Lister (197 and 196). They had shown signs of dissociating themselves before from the Lancashire Tories: see above, p. 11. Both were included in the list of 'Justices thought fit to be turned out' of 10 Sept. 1696: Hist. MSS. Comm., *Kenyon MSS.*, 411.

[5] Farrer (3) later became king's counsel and receiver general for Cambridgeshire: Walcott, *English Politics*, 175.

[6] England and Fuller (233 and 234) had been in negotiation with the Admiralty on behalf of the town since the beginning of the parliament. By 26 November, the negotiations had reached their final stages and it is very likely that they thought it advisable to support the government at this point. Their correspondence with the corporation was kindly made available to us by the Town Clerk of Great Yarmouth.

Whigs, have been expected to vote against the bill, but nevertheless supported it.[1]

From the evidence of this division list it is clear that the effect of the Fenwick affair on normal party ties has been exaggerated. There was a small but significant defection from the ranks of the Court and the division also reflected the general shift of members' allegiance since the early weeks of the new parliament—Court Tories into opposition and new, uncommitted members to the Court. But the great mass of members followed the same party line upon the attainder as they had done upon the two very different issues of the council of trade and the price of guineas—a striking testimony to the importance of party politics in William III's reign.

[1]Thomas Foley (436) does not seem to have shared fully the family enthusiasm for opposition. He had disagreed with his son, Thomas, and his brother, Paul, over the abjuration oath in 1692. His humiliating defeat at the county polls in 1698 was attributed by at least one contemporary to his support for the Court. See Hist. MSS. Comm., *Portland MSS.*, iii, 510, and Brit. Mus., Add MS. 29579, ff. 44–6. Among Walcott's closest family connection there was, seemingly, a black sheep.

Analysis of the Lists

IT HAS SEEMED to the present authors that the existence of these three lists, all compiled within the year 1696, presented a good opportunity to classify members of parliament as narrowly as possible according to their appearance on the lists. A purely mechanical classification taking into account only their record according to the three lists seemed the most likely way of establishing conclusions of statistical validity free from the element of subjective impression which is not necessarily more reliable for being contemporary. This mechanical classification has been taken as a member's political allegiance for the year 1696. Once arrived at, the classification has been compared with, first of all, every known list for the reign of William III. For the period subsequent to 1696, the classification has been simplified to one of *Whig* or *Tory* or, for a handful of members, *uncertain*. This information has been tabulated in Appendix A to which a key is provided.[1] Members are listed in the conventional order of constituencies and numbered according to this order for ease of reference. Those members of the 1695–6 parliament who continued to sit into Anne's reign are further listed in Appendix B. In this section they have been divided according to their final classification of *Whig*, *Tory* (subdivided into *Moderate* and *High*) and *Uncertain*. This classification has then been compared with all known lists of Anne's reign. A key to this section is also given.[2] Although some of the members continued to sit after 1714, they have been thought to be too few on which to base any further argument.

The information used in this analysis seemed at the outset to be of various kinds. Some of the lists purported to be actual division lists; others were simply statements of the general attitude of members. The reliability of none of the lists could be taken for granted. Yet investigation showed that both the diversity and the likely unreliability of the lists had been exaggerated. Even lists purporting to be division lists often failed, like the guineas list, to correspond at all to the figures of the actual division, and it is likely that many (though not all) were as much statements of the general attitude of members as were lists such as those of Grascombe and that of the parliament of 1710 which record the general position of members of the House. As for reliability, it was found in practice that either the lists corresponded very well with what other evidence would have led one to expect, or else, in the case of one or two such as the lists of those opposing the tack, and the compilation of members' religious attitudes in the parliament of 1705, they were so blatantly inaccurate that it was proper to discount them entirely. Much less reliance would have to be placed on the evidence of the

[1] See pp. 40 ff.
[2] See pp. 53 ff.

lists if there were fewer of them or if their results were less consistent than they have proved to be. As it is, when considered in their entirety, they all point one way, and in so doing, establish both a conclusion and their own validity.

We have been concerned in this analysis with, in all, 512 members of the parliament elected in November 1695. Five hundred and four of these members are those who appear on the council of trade list and a further eight appear in either or both of the lists on the price of guineas and the attainder of Fenwick.

The rules adopted for classification on the basis of the three lists of 1696 may be open to some criticism but are probably as objective as any such system of classification is likely to be. Appearance on either the coinage list or the list on the attainder of Fenwick has been taken to be a clear vote for one side or the other. The council of trade list, falling into another category of evidence, was taken to need special rules. Inclusion in the *Pro* or *Con* column of the main list has been taken as evidence of allegiance. Those appearing in the *D*[oubtful] column (D in column 3) have been ignored unless they were further classified on the front sheet, in which case these further classifications have been accepted as the equivalent of *Pro* or *Con* in the main list (Dc and Do in column 3).

Classification on the three lists of 1696 has been carried out on the following basis. Members who appear on two or three of the lists have been classified as either *Court* (C) or *Opposition* (O), if those votes were consistent. Those with only one appearance have been classified as either *probably Court* (pC) or *probably Opposition* (pO). If a member's only appearance is in the council of trade list as *D*[oubtful], he has been classified as *Uncertain* (U). Those with two or three appearances which were not consistent have been classified as *inconsistent* (i).

The *inconsistent* voters clearly required further classification. Those with three votes fall into three easily distinguishable groups. The largest consists of those who begin the year in opposition to the Court but subsequently change sides. Some had changed by the time the struggle over the price of guineas had ended; others not until the vote on Fenwick's attainder. Those who begin the year in support of the Court but subsequently desert it for the opposition comprise a smaller group divided into two distinct parts: those who desert only upon the issue of Fenwick, and the hitherto Court Tories who go into permanent opposition after refusing to sign the Association. Finally there is a third group whose behaviour seems eccentric. They were in opposition over the council of trade, supported the Court over the price of guineas, and finally go back into opposition on the occasion of Fenwick's attainder. This political course is exactly that followed by the Duke of Leeds, and the presence among this group of persons readily recognisable as the duke's political associates identifies it as comprising his personal following in the Commons. Thus, all the members with three appearances in 1696, one of which was inconsistent, may be classified according to their records as follows:

Record in 1696			Classification
Trade	Guineas	Fenwick	
O (or Do)	O or C	C	*Court Convert* (iV)
C (or Dc)	C	O	*Fenwick Independent* (iF)
C (or Dc)	O	O	*Ex-Court Tory* (iX)[1]
O (or Do)	C	O	*Leeds Tory* (iL)

However, not all members have their allegiance recorded for all three occasions and their absence from one may make it necessary to go outside these lists of 1696 to determine their classification, and even then it may only prove possible to ascribe a 'probable' classification.

In some cases a member's absence creates no difficulties. A man who supports the Court on Fenwick's attainder and opposes it on either the council of trade or the price of guineas must be a *Court Convert* (iV). Since no one voted Court, Opposition, Court, on the three issues, and there appears to be no good reason why anyone should have done so, it seems reasonable to suppose that anyone with the record for 1696 of absent, Opposition, Court, would have been in sympathy with the opposition on the first issue. Alternatively, a record of Opposition on the council of trade, absent on the price of guineas and Court on Fenwick, also classifies a man as *Court Convert*.

Outside the three lists of 1696, three other criteria have been used when the evidence of 1696 is deficient: whether the member was listed as a Court supporter by Grascombe in 1693–4 (shown by C in column 8), whether he refused to sign the Association (* in column 9) and whether he is known to have been an associate of the Duke of Leeds.

A member appearing as Court on the council of trade, Opposition on the price of guineas and absent on Fenwick is classed as *Ex-Court Tory* (iX) if[2] he refuses the Association and as *Uncertain* (iU) if he signs it.[3] If a man is listed as Court on the council of trade, absent on the price of guineas and Opposition on Fenwick's attainder he is classed as *Ex-Court Tory* (iX) if he refuses the Association and *probably Fenwick Independent* (ipF) if he signs it. A record of Opposition on the council of trade, Court on the price of guineas and absent on Fenwick's attainder classes a member as *probably Leeds Tory* (ipL) if he was listed by Grascombe as a Court supporter or is known to have been a close associate of Leeds,[4] and as *probably Court Convert* (ipV) if neither, unless he refuses the Association when he is classed as *Uncertain* (iU).[5] The following table summarises these further classifications for convenience:

[1] Also refused the Association.

[2] In fact, only three had this record: 152, 240 and 377.

[3] John Lewknor (378) is the one member relegated to the limbo of *inconsistent Uncertain* on this score.

[4] Only James Herbert (20), Leeds's son-in-law, is classified by this criterion alone; Charles Osborne (449), Leeds's son, is classified by Grascombe's having listed him as a Court supporter in 1693–4.

[5] Sir William Trumbull (266) is the one member who falls into this unlikely

Record in 1696			*Other qualification*	*Classification*
Trade	*Guineas*	*Fenwick*		
absent (or D)	O	C	—	*Court Convert* (iV)
O (or Do)	absent	C	—	*Court Convert* (iV)
O (or Do)	C	absent	Court in Grascombe list	*prob. Leeds Tory* (ipL)
O (or Do)	C	absent	Leeds's associate	*prob. Leeds Tory* (ipL)
O (or Do)	C	absent	signed Association	*prob. Court Convert* (ipV)
O (or Do)	C	absent	refused Association[1]	*Uncertain* (iU)
C (or Dc)	absent	O	signed Association[2]	*prob. Fenwick Independent* (ipF)
C (or Dc)	O	absent	refused Association	*Ex-Court Tory* (iX)
C (or Dc)	O	absent	signed Association	*Uncertain* (iU)

In January 1696, 248 M.P.s[3] can be counted as Court supporters, 247 as opposition supporters, and nine as being of uncertain allegiance. These can be divided, according to the system of classification adopted here, as follows:

Court		*Opposition*		*Uncertain*	
C	199	O	175	U	8
pC	32	pO	34	iU	2
iF	6	iL	4		10
ipF	6	ipL	6		
iX	5	iV	23		
	248	ipV	5		
			247		

One hundred and thirty-eight of these members are recorded as voting Whig or Tory on the issues of 1689 (column 7: the making of the Prince and Princess of Orange king and queen, and the Sacheverell clause which would have effected a Whig purge of the municipal corporations). In 1696 the allegiance of these 138 members was as follows:

Court		*Opposition*		*Uncertain*	
Whigs in 1689	65	Whigs in 1689	13	Whig in 1689	1
Tories in 1689	5	Tories in 1689	53		
		Both Whig and Tory in 1689	1		

category. It is realised that the tests used here are not ideally satisfactory. Thus, not all the firm *Leeds Tories* are listed as Court supporters by Grascombe, and Grascombe lists as Court supporters some of the firm *Court Converts*, but it is claimed that there is a marked contrast between the records of the two groups—Grascombe lists four out of five firm *Leeds Tories* as Court supporters and only five out of twenty-three firm *Court Converts*—for this test to be objective and effective in selecting from members with incomplete voting records those whose voting behaviour *probably* followed that of the Duke of Leeds.

[1] Being neither Court in the Grascombe list nor an associate of the Duke of Leeds.

[2] Had any members with this record in 1696 refused to sign the Association, they would have been classified as *Ex-Court Tories*, but in fact none did so.

[3] This out of a total of 505, Sir Rowland Gwynn having been added to the 504 members listed in the council of trade forecast.

The small number of Tories supporting the government (if the *Leeds Tories* had continued to support the Court the number of 1689 Tories on that side would have been increased by three) and the substantial number of Whigs supporting the opposition are both remarkable, and they lend considerable support to Feiling's thesis that in 1696 Harley was seeking to form a new party out of Tories and Country Whigs.

Grascombe's 1693–4 list of the Court supporters in the parliament of 1690 (column 8) includes 128 of the members of January 1696. Of these, 107 are still Court supporters in January 1696; of the rest, eight are *Leeds Tories* (Court supporters when Grascombe compiled his list), ten are opposition supporters other than *Leeds Tories*, and the allegiance of the other three is uncertain. The correlation between the Grascombe list and the 1696 classification is therefore 92·0 per cent (115 out of 125), and it is further remarkable that five of the ten opposition supporters go over to the Court during the course of 1696, which suggests that their temporary adherence to the opposition in January 1696 ought not to be held to contradict Grascombe's identification of them as Court supporters in the 1690 parliament. Of the remaining five members won over from the Court by Harley, two are recorded as Tories in 1689,[1] and of the other three, one died in 1696 while another returned to full Whig allegiance under Anne;[2] it would seem that he succeeded in winning over virtually no members who were not Country Whigs or Tories.[3]

Grascombe also includes in his list nineteen of the 1696 members as holding an office or pension in spite of which they were not Court supporters. Only seven of these had become Court supporters by January 1696, a fact which suggests that while the holding of a place or the receipt of a pension might draw a man to support the Court, it was not an overriding factor in the determination of his political allegiance in this period. Of those Grascombe appears to exclude from his list ('O' in column 8), only nine supported the Court in January 1696 while eighty-nine opposed it, the allegiance of two being uncertain. The correlation here is 90·8 per cent (eighty-nine out of ninety-eight).

By the time of the decisive votes on the price of guineas, the political grouping had changed. On this issue, the *Leeds Tories* supported the Court, the *Ex-Court Tories* had gone into opposition, and at least fifteen—possibly up to five more—opposition supporters had been converted to the Court. In addition, two Court supporters had left the House while two new members, one Court and one opposition, sat for the first time. In consequence of these changes, the Court's theoretical majority had increased from one to between thirty-nine and forty-nine, the groups being made up as follows according to our classification:

[1] Gilbert Dolben (241) and Philip Bickerstaffe (249).

[2] Thomas Lewes (19) and William Carr (251).

[3] Even the fifth member, William Hayn (113) is a slightly doubtful addition to Harley's following: he cast no votes after the council of trade divisions and he is marked for that occasion with a faint red dot.

Court		*Opposition*		*Uncertain*	
C	199	O	175	U	8
pC	31	pO	35	iU	2
iF, ipF	12	iX	5		10
iL, ipL	10	iV, ipV	8 to 13		
iV, ipV	15 to 20		223 to 228		
	267 to 272				

By the end of the year, the *Leeds Tories* had returned to opposition whilst all the *Court Converts* had left it; five new M.P.s had arrived, four of them Court supporters, while ten old ones had departed, three of them Court, and seven opposition, supporters. The Court's theoretical majority was now therefore fifty-two, made up as follows:

Court		*Opposition*		*Uncertain*	
C	197	O	171	U	8
pC	34	pO	33	iU	2
iV, ipV	28	iX	5		10
iF, ipF	12	iL, ipL	10		
	271		219		

But over the issue of Fenwick's attainder the defection of twelve *Fenwick Independents* reduced the Court total to 259 and, correspondingly, raised the opposition total by twelve to 231. This reduced the Court's theoretical majority to twenty-eight, but for that issue only.

These calculated theoretical majorities for the three issues of 1696 correspond favourably with the majorities actually recorded:

	Council of Trade	*Price of Guineas*	*Fenwick*
Calculated majority	1	39–49	28
Actual majority	−21, −7	47	33

The greatest discrepancy is on the council of trade but on this occasion the balance of red emendations to the list and contemporary comment both suggest that the government performance was worse than expectation.

It is not the purpose of this analysis to write a definitive history of party between 1689 and 1714, but to provide some statistical information to that end, and to advance some propositions which the evidence we have collected seems to suggest. With respect to 1696 it is our contention that the fusion of Tory and Country elements to form a new Tory party led by Harley until his fall in 1714, which Feiling first propounded in 1924[1] must now for the most part be accepted as a well documented fact. Harley was probably not as successful as he would have wished to be in attracting Country Whigs to his side. Only three out of fourteen Whigs who supported

[1]Feiling, 314–16.

him in January subsequently deserted to the Court, but the other twenty-five *Court Converts* had a high proportion of new members without office whose continued support would undoubtedly have been welcome. On the other hand Harley had great success in recruiting former Court Tories. Twenty-three of his supporters were placemen, and almost all of them can be identified as Tories: nine are classed as *Leeds Tories*, six refused to sign the Association, two more are recorded as Tories in 1689, while a further three, Charles Trelawny (60), George Churchill (169) and Edmund Webb (424) are known to have been Tories.[1] Ninety-five of his supporters refused to sign the Association which none of the Court supporters did.[2] What happened in 1696 therefore was the virtual completion of the process whereby a House of Commons divided into Court and Country parties, each with its Whig and Tory members, has been replaced by one in which Whig and Court on the one hand, and Tory and Country on the other, are synonymous terms. Only the group of Leeds Tories constitute for a short period an exception to this rule when, on the issue of the disbanding of the standing army, a majority of them behave like the Court supporters they had once been (and the placemen many of them still were) instead of as the outright Tories they were to become. With this exception, all Court supporters at the end of 1696 have therefore been treated as Whigs from that date, and all supporters of the opposition as Tories (column 13).

Four hundred and fifty of the members sitting at the end of 1696 appear on the list of the 1698 Parliament which classifies members according to their attitude towards the standing army,[3] and 102 of these appear in the list of members opposing the disbanding of the standing army in the division of 1699 (column 10). They may be analysed into Whig and Tory according to the definition just given as follows:

[1]The other three are John Backwell (25), Sir Robert Cotton (34) and William Coward (294).

[2]Sir William Trumbull (266) classified as *Uncertain* is the only other member to refuse the Association.

[3]We would identify the purpose of the important list discovered by Dr. Henry Horwitz as concerned with the disbanding of the standing army for these reasons: (i) It was expected to be, and it proved to be, *the* controversial issue of the opening weeks of the 1698 Parliament when this list was compiled. (ii) It was the only such issue which had been a first rate political issue also in the last session of the 1695–8 Parliament and for which therefore information could exist for assessing together the attitudes of retiring, continuing and new members, and the only issue for which such an assessment could prove useful. (iii) The Leeds Tories support the Court 6 to 3 on this list, and the disbanding of the standing army is the last major issue upon which they are known to support the Court. (iv) Five members, numbers 60, 61, 132, 169 and 299, are listed as Court supporters on this list, yet according to their 1696 record they are Tories and they follow a Tory line upon at least two of the following three issues: opposition to war preparations in 1701 (list 11), the impeachment of William III's ministers (list 12), and the election of the Speaker in 1705 (Appendix B list 7); four of the five however are listed as supporters of the standing army in 1699 (marked * in list 10) and all except number 132 were senior army officers in 1698. (v) Upon no other issue could the support for the Court of Sir Richard Onslow (357) be in doubt at this time.

	For the Standing Army in 1698	*Against the Standing Army in 1698*	*For the Standing Army in 1699*
Whigs and Leeds Tories	227	25	92
Tories excluding Leeds Tories	25	164	8
Uncertain	4	5	2

The classification of 1696, therefore, provides an 88·7 per cent accurate forecast (391 out of 441) of the members' attitudes in 1698 and a 92·0 per cent accurate forecast (92 out of 100) of their voting behaviour in 1699.

The two remaining divisions of William III's reign (columns 11 and 12) list 161 votes cast by the opposition. According to the 1696 classification, 151 of the members casting these votes are Tories, 9 are Whigs, and 1 is Uncertain: it is therefore a 94·4 per cent accurate forecast (151 out of 160) for these divisions.

Appendix B lists the votes of 104 Whigs, 109 Tories and three M.P.s of uncertain allegiance who appear in one or more of the divisions and party lists of Anne's reign. In two of the divisions, that over the Lords' amendments to the Act enlarging the time for taking the Oath of Abjuration, 1703, and that on the impeachment of Sacheverell, 1709, the issue involved went beyond consideration of support or opposition to the Court and raised the fundamental differences between Whig and Tory that went back to 1689 and beyond. These two divisions (columns 3 and 4) have therefore been considered separately from the rest as referring to the basic conviction of members, and with them has been put the descriptive list of the 1710 parliament (column 5) which clearly describes members in the same terms. In these three lists, the Whigs of 1696 register 124 Whig and eight Tory votes, while the Tories of 1696 register 137 Tory and eighteen Whig votes.[1] The 1696 classification is thus shown to be 91·0 per cent accurate (261 out of 287) for the reign of Queen Anne, even without being modified, as it should be, to take account of persons known to have changed their basic political allegiance between 1696 and 1702.

Any analysis of the eight divisions in which the issue is principally one involving support for, or opposition to, the government, is complicated by the fact that up to 1708 the Court is supported by both Whigs and Tories. It is necessary, therefore, to be able to distinguish among the Tories between those who were prepared up to 1708 to support the government, who may, for convenience, be called *Moderate Tories*, and those who were not, who may be called *High Tories*, before we are in a position to test the accuracy of the 1696 forecast for these years. Fortunately there is accurate contemporary information enabling us to distinguish between the two

[1] In addition, those classified as *Uncertain* in 1696 register six Whig votes and four *Whigs* of 1696 are marked as 'Doubtful' for the Parliament of 1710.

groups. In the division list showing votes cast in the election of the Speaker in 1705 marks were made against those voting for the Court candidate who were considered to be Tories. These marks pick out sixteen of the classified members of 1696 as *Moderate Tories* according to our definition, and this identification has been accepted with two amendments: William Lowndes (489) and Thomas Foley (165). Lowndes was marked as a Tory on the Speaker's list. Perhaps this properly describes his fundamental political sympathies, but he was throughout this period Secretary of the Treasury and the senior civil servant of the day, so that his 1696 classification of Whig is probably the more accurate description of his voting behaviour, although ultimately he is not definable within any general category. He has therefore been left a Whig in this analysis. Foley has been added to the list of *Moderate Tories*, although not marked as a Tory on the Speaker's list, on the ground of his being a very close associate of Harley. These two changes leave the number of members classified as *Moderate Tories* at sixteen.

In the three divisions occurring in the period up to 1708 (columns 6–8), 174 votes were cast for the Court and ninety-five for the opposition, as follows:

	For the Court	*For the opposition*
Whigs	126	8
Moderate Tories	29	0
High Tories	14	87
Uncertain	5	0

The crude 1696 classification (that is, not corrected for changes in basic political allegiance between 1696 and 1702) is therefore 91·7 per cent accurate (242 out of 264). In the single division of the parliament of 1708–10 when an exclusively Whig ministry governed, fifty-eight votes, all for the Court, were cast by forty-eight Whigs, one *Moderate Tory*, six *High Tories*, and three members classified in 1696 as *Uncertain*, showing the crude 1696 classification to be 87·3 per cent accurate (forty-eight out of fifty-five). In the four divisions after 1710 under a Tory ministry, thirty votes were cast for the Court and sixty-eight for the opposition as follows:

	For the Court	*For the opposition*
Whigs	5	50
Moderate Tories	8	0
High Tories	17	13
Uncertain	0	5

The unmodified 1696 classification is therefore 80·6 per cent accurate (seventy-five out of ninety-three).

The substantial accuracy, on average about 90 per cent, of the 1696 classification is apparent. That it is not a 100 per cent accurate forecast will be due, apart from errors in the original lists or inaccuracies introduced by the present authors, to one or both of two causes: either some members did not vote consistently according to a basic party allegiance, or the basic party allegiance of some members had changed between 1696 and 1702. The latter possibility can be tested by examining the total records of all members under Anne to discover whether there are any members with a substantial voting record that is inconsistent with their existing classification but perfectly consistent with an alternative one. There are, in fact, seven such members, an examination of whose voting record under Anne (see appendices) makes it plain that their classification should be modified as follows:

	1696 classification	*New classification*
Henry Boyle (31)	Tory (O)	Whig
Henry Vincent (47)	Tory (O)	Whig
Peregrine Bertie (208)	Tory (iL)	Whig
William Carr (251)	Tory (O)	Whig
Sir Henry Belasyse (253)	Whig (iV)	High Tory
John Webb (428)	Whig (pC)	Moderate Tory
Arthur Owen (509)	Tory (O)	Whig

In addition, three members who, in 1696, were of uncertain allegiance, can be classified under Anne with absolute certainty as Whigs.

Three of the persons apparently wrongly classified, Henry Boyle, Peregrine Bertie and Sir Henry Belasyse, are known to have changed their political allegiance after 1696, and it is probable that when Henry Vincent became a placeman under Anne he did the same. John Webb seems to have been an error in classification in 1696, his whiggery depending on a single mark of *Pro* on the council of trade list that had originally classified him as *D*[oubtful].[1] We have no explanation to offer for the failure of William Carr and Arthur Owen to behave according to their classifications. We have accepted, for Anne's reign, a revised classification for all seven members, and in addition for the three members originally classified as *Uncertain*. According to this revised classification the voting record of the three parties under Anne is as follows:

	Whigs	*Moderate Tories*	*High Tories*
(Appendix B, columns 3–5)			
Voting as Whigs	141	4	3
Voting as Tories	5	24	116
95·9% accurate (281 out of 293)			

[1] For Henry Boyle see Onslow's note to Burnet's *History of his Own Time* (6 vols., Oxford, 1823), v, 345. General Belasyse was courtmartialed and disgraced for his conduct on the Cadiz expedition of 1702. Peregrine Bertie was a Danby follower who retained his sinecures and allowed his political behaviour to become indistinguishable from that of a Whig. John Richmond Webb was the victor of the battle of Wynendael in 1708 who was removed from the army as a Jacobite in 1715; his father, Colonel Edmund Webb (424) was a cousin of Henry St. John and Walcott (*English Politics*, 68) classifies both father and son as Harley Tories in 1701; not unnaturally, both were expected to support the Court over the standing army in 1698.

	Whigs	*Moderate Tories*	*High Tories*
Up to 1708 (Appendix B, columns 6–8)			
For the Court	136	30	8
For the opposition	6	0	89
94·8% accurate (255 out of 269)			
1708–10 (Appendix B, column 9)			
For the Court	55	1	2
94·8% accurate (55 out of 58)			
After 1710 (Appendix B, columns 10–13)			
For the Court	4	9	17
For the opposition	56	0	12
83·7% accurate (82 out of 98)			

The general accuracy of the classification is 93·7 per cent (673 out of 718).

Once account has been taken of changes in political allegiance between 1696 and 1702, very little erratic voting remains and the conclusion must be reached that voting behaviour after 1696 and up to 1714 is governed almost entirely by party allegiance. The proposition that a fundamental shift in political structure had taken place by the end of 1696, and that henceforth the House of Commons was divided into Whig and Tory rather than into Court and Country, is amply supported by the evidence of the division lists. Nor can the substantial accuracy of these lists be any longer doubted.

In addition to this main conclusion, it seems that some tentative propositions can be suggested from the evidence of the lists and divisions in Anne's reign. First it seems that the *Moderate Tories* formed a clearly defined group distinct from both Whigs and *High Tories* and constituting a substantial proportion of the government's strength up to 1708. It is notable that only two of them refused the Association in 1696.

The second of these tentative propositions is that there seems to have been no substantial Court group independent of the parties. There is certainly very little evidence so far for the existence of any such group but the evidence for the periods of Tory government is not as full as one would like it to be. There is no Court list for the parliament of 1702–5, and only the exceptional list for the French Commercial Treaty for the parliaments of 1710–14. Nor have we any list dealing with the vital session of 1707–8 to test the validity of a distinction at that time between Court and other Whigs. Such evidence as does exist points with certainty only to William Lowndes (489) and possibly to Robert Monckton (473). On the other hand, the gain or loss of office appears to have been a factor in most of the fundamental changes of allegiance between 1696 and 1702.

A further point is that there is only scattered evidence for the existence of Walcott's personal groupings. Robert Monckton (473), a follower of the Duke of Newcastle, Harley's Whig ally, is a Whig supporter of the French Commercial Treaty, while two of the Tories opposing that treaty, Peter Shakerley (195) and James Bertie (270), are followers of Harley's Tory opponent, the Earl of Nottingham. It is possible that the irregular records of John Aislaby (454) and William Pierrepont (258) owe something to a connection with Nottingham. Only the Duke of Leeds's twelve members in 1696 form a substantial group, and it is hardly likely that *his* following, the result of a deliberate policy while at the head of affairs under two sovereigns, was a typical one. It may be hazarded that personal groupings were small and operated largely within the basic party divisions.

There is, on the other hand, some evidence that such erratic voting as did occur stemmed from the actions of members in a position to act independently of their own volition. Charles Godfrey (18), Marlborough's brother-in-law, Russell Robartes (49), Lord Radnor's brother, and Sir Philip Boteler (480), were all men of substance capable of taking an independent line. So, in another way, were merchants such as Arthur Champneys (102) and William Johnson (350). Nevertheless, the considerable accuracy of our classification indicates that whatever factors influenced members to take an independent course, the part they played in the political life of this period must have been very small.

Two qualifications ought to be made concerning the conclusions from this analysis. First, since the analysis has been made mechanically, deliberately in order to provide a strictly objective test of the strength of party ties and of the accuracy of the lists themselves, it contains some anomalies which the authors would wish to correct in the light of other evidence were they drawing up a party classification of the members of 1696. The mechanical classification, for instance, provides little evidence for the Country Whig antecedents of Robert Harley and his new Country group. Sir William Trumbull would be another member whose attitude it would be desirable to define more closely than *inconsistent Uncertain*. But the striking thing is the small number of such anomalies considering the fine distinctions that have had to be drawn in order to make the classification cover as many members as possible. Only in the case of the Court Tories does the evidence of the analysis appear to require further explanation.

There were undoubtedly Court Tories in the parliamentary session of 1695–6 and it is interesting to compare the generally accepted impression of these Court Tories with the results of our mechanical classification. Our classification produces two types of Court Tory: those we have labelled *Ex-Court Tory* and those we have styled *Leeds Tories*. The group of *Ex-Court Tories* comprises five members only who, according to our rules, could not be classified in any other way. All were listed as Court on the council of trade list and all subsequently went with the opposition. There is little evidence to show any strong personal commitment to the Court save in the case of Henry Holmes (313), who was Governor of Hurst Castle, and probably they comprise a group of Tories disposed to support the Court rather than a group of Tory placemen. Our group of *Leeds Tories* is based on their voting pattern which reproduces the known attitude of the Duke of Leeds. Some of the group are undoubtedly accurately described by this title, Charles Osborne, for example, with James Herbert and the Berties.[1] In other instances, there is no direct evidence, apart from the voting pattern, to connect the members so classified with Leeds. Edward and George Nicholas (132 and 252) would fall into this class.[2] But they were all Tories still connected in some measure with the Court by virtue of holding places and it may be that they shared a common outlook and common ties with Leeds who was in much the same position. Most, like Leeds himself, broke finally with the Court by 1699 but a minority, like Peregrine Bertie, persisted in office and became indistinguishable from Whigs.

The followers of Godolphin, sometimes taken as being by definition Court Tories, are with one exception, according to our classification list, among the main body of the Whigs in much the same way as Harley's Country Whig following is indistinguishable from the Tories. The exception is Francis Godolphin (50). It is possible that the line between him and Charles Godolphin (51) is drawn too finely, Francis being classified on his 1696 record as *probably Opposition* whilst Charles is *Court*. Nevertheless their behaviour, for whatever reason, was different, and has to be taken into account. In fact, the mechanical classification as Whig of those usually looked on as followers or connections of Godolphin, and who are listed by Walcott as members of his interest, is probably an instance in which our method produces a result more in keeping with political reality than the evidence of gossip, rumour or even Godolphin's self-delusion. Godolphin's own actual behaviour, on the same grounds, would be classifiable as Whig since, whatever public or private reservations he might have made, he acted in accordance with Whig principles.

Secondly, it has to be admitted that the failure of any division lists to record deliberate abstentions as distinct from mere absence may well conceal the most important departures from party voting. There is evidence, in the council of trade list for instance, that in 1696 abstention rather than cross voting was the solution adopted to resolve any conflict between party claims and other pressure. However, this may be a product of the transitional state of parties in this year.

Finally, we do not contend in any way that the conclusions offered are definitive, but we do maintain that they are so well established by this form of analysis as to demand acceptance in default of evidence to the contrary.

[1] See p. 11. [2] See p. 25.

APPENDIX A

The Voting Record of Members in 1696 and during the Reign of William III

KEY

The List or Lists used in compiling the Appendix are indicated in this Key. Further information about these lists and about other copies of them is given by R. Walcott and E. S. de Beer in their articles in *B.I.H.R.*, xiv (1936), 25–36 and xix (1942), 65–6.

Column:

1 The number of the seat in conventional order.

2 The name of the member sitting on 31 January 1696 according to the *Official Return of Members of the House of Commons*. Members not included in the Council of Trade List have their names in italic type. Members returned after 31 January are added at the end with the suffix 'b' after the number of their seat.

3 The Council of Trade List, 1696 (see above, p. 7):
C = *Pro.*
Dc = *Doubtful*, but classified as *Pro* on the front sheet.
O = *Con.*
Do = *Doubtful*, but classified as *Con* on the front sheet.
D = *Doubtful*, and not classified on the front sheet.

4 The Price of Guineas List, 1696 (see above, p. 17):
C = *Yea.*
O = *No.*

5 The Attainder of Fenwick List, 1696 (see above, p. 23):
C = *For.*
O = *Against.*

6 Classification according to voting behaviour in 1696 (see above pp. 28–30).

7 Political allegiance in 1689:
T = Tory, opposed to making the Prince and Princess of Orange king and queen (Feiling, 496–8).
W = Whig, in favour of the 'Sacheverell Clause' excluding Tories from office in municipal corporations (J. Oldmixon, *The History of England* (1735), 36–7).

8 Grascombe's list of the 1690 parliament ('A List of members of the House of Commons marked respectively with the letters C, O, CO, CP, OP, and COP', Bodl. Libr., MS. Rawl. D. 846, f. 5):
C = Court supporter, marked on the list with a 'C' with or without another letter.

OP=Placeman or pensioner but not Court supporter, marked on the list with 'O', 'P', or 'OP', but not with 'C'.
O=Opposition supporter, not included in the list although a member at the time it was compiled.

9 P=Placeman in 1696 (information collected by the present authors).
*=refused to sign the Association at first (Browning, *Danby*, iii, 194–213).

10 The disbanding of the standing army, 1697–9:

(a) The list of the parliament of 1698 and of members of the parliament of 1695 not re-elected in 1698 (Horwitz, 62–9; Dr. Horwitz does not identify this list with the issue of the standing army; our reasons for doing so appear in p. 33 n. 3 above):
C= Supporter of a standing army, marked on the list '×' or '+'.
O=Opposed to a standing army, marked on the list '√'.
q=Uncertain attitude to the standing army, marked on the list other than as above.

(b) *=Against the disbanding of the army in 1699 (Browning, *Danby*, iii, 213–17); an alternative version to that used by Browning adds numbers 145, 211, 323 and 448 (copy supplied to the History of Parliament by Prof. Basil Henning).

11 O=Opposed to making preparations for war in 1701 (*Somers Tracts*, xii, 212–15).

12 O=In favour of the impeachment of William III's ministers in 1702 (*Somers Tracts*, xii, 215–18).

13 Party allegiance after 1696 determined according to the voting record of that year (column 6):
W=Whig T=Tory U=Uncertain

1	2	3	4	5	6	7	8	9	10	11	12	13
	Bedfordshire:											
1	Edw. Ld. Russell	C	C	C	C	W	C	P	C*			W
2	Wm. Duncombe	O	O		O	W			O			T
3	Wm. Farrer	D	O	C	iV				C			W
4	Thos. Hillersdon	C			pC		C					W
	Berkshire:											
5	Ric. Nevile	C	C	C	C				C*			W
6	Sir Humphrey Foster	O	O	O	O		O		O			T
7	Jn. Vis. Fitzharding	C	C		C		C	P	C*			W
8	Sir Wm. Scawen	C	C	C	C				C*			W
9	Sir Wm. Rich	C	C	C	C	W	C		C*			W
10	Sir Henry Fane	C	C		C	W	C		C			W
11	Wm. Jennens	O	O		O		O	*	O	O	O	T
12	Thos. Tipping	C	C		C	W		P	C*			W
13	Simon Harcourt	O	O	O	O		O	*	O	O	O	T
	Buckinghamshire:											
14	Thos. Wharton	C	C	to HoL	C	W	C	P				W
15	Sir Ric. Atkyns	C	C		C			P				W
16	Sir Ric. Temple	O	O	O	O		OP					T
17	Alex. Denton	O	O	O	O		O	*	O			T

1	2	3	4	5	6	7	8	9	10	11	12	13
18	Chas. Godfrey	C	C	C	C	W	C	P	C*			W
19	Thos. Lewes	O		*Died*	pO	W	C					T
20	Jas. Herbert	O	C		ipL			P	O	O	O	T
21	Sir Thos. Lee	C	C	C	C	W	C		C*			W
22	Montague Drake	O	O	O	O			*				T
23	Edmund Waller	O	O	O	O		O		O			T
24	Ric. Beke	C	C		C		C	P	C*			W
25	Jn. Backwell	O	O	O	O		O	P	O	O		T
26	Sir Jas. Etheredge	O	O	O	O			*	O	O	O	T
27	Jas. Chase	C	C	C	C		OP	P	C*			W
	Cambridgeshire:											
28	Jn. Ld. Cutts	C	C	C	C			P	C*			W
29	Edw. Russell	C	C	C	C	W	C	P				W
30	Geo. Oxenden	O	C	C	iV			P	C			W
31	Henry Boyle	O	O	O	O	W	O		C*			T
32	Jn. Pepys	O	O	*Died*	O							T
33	Isaac Watlington	O	O	O	O				O			T
	Cheshire:											
34	Sir Robt. Cotton	O	O	O	O	W	O	P	O			T
35	Sir Jn. Mainwaring	C	C	C	C	W	C		C*			W
36	Roger Whitley	C			pC	W		P				W
37	Sir Thos. Grosvenor	Do	O	O	O		O	*	O			T
	Cornwall:											
38	Jn. Specot	O	O		O	T	O		O			T
39	Hugh Boscawen	C	C	C	C	W	OP	P	C*			W
40	Henry Ld. Hide	O	O	O	O		O	*	O	O	O	T
41	Wm. Cary	O		O	O	T	O		O		O	T
42	Sir Bourchier Wray	O		*Died*	pO	T	OP					T
43	Wm. Bridges	O			pO				C		O	T
44	Sam. Travers	C	C	C	C		C	P	C*			W
45	Bernard Granville	O	O	O	O		OP	*	C			T
46	Jn. Cloberye	C		C	C				C			W
47	Henry Vincent	O		O	O		O		C			T
48	Jn. Hoblyn	O	O	O	O				O	O	O	T
49	Russell Robartes	C	C	C	C				C			W
50	Fras. Godolphin	D		O	pO				C			T
51	Chas. Godolphin	Dc	C		C	T	C	P	C	O		W
52	Fras. Buller	O	O	O	O			*				T
53	Walter Moyle	C	C	C	C				O			W
54	Robt. Molesworth	C	C	C	C				C			W
55	Ambrose Manaton[1]	O		*Died*	pO		O					T
56	Jas. Kendall	O	C	C	iV			P	C*			W
57	Jas. Mount Stephens	O		O	O			*	O	O		T
58	Hugh Fortescue	C	C	C	C	W	C		C*			W
59	Jn. Tanner	O			pO	T	OP		O			T
60	Chas. Trelawny	O	O		O		O	P	C*	O	O	T
61	Henry Trelawny	O	C		ipL		C	P	C*	O		T
62	Jas. Vernon	C	C	C	C			P	C*			W
63	Alex. Pendarves	O	O		O	T	O			O	O	T
64	Fras. Robarts	O	C		ipV	T	OP	P	C			W
65	Jas. Montagu	C	C	C	C							W
66	Geo. Boothe	C	C	C	C		C		C*			W
67	Jn. Manley	O	O	O	O			P*	O		O	T
68	Jn. Michel	C			pC		C		O			W
69	Jas. Praed	O			pO	T	O		O			T
70	Thos. Vivian	O			pO				C			T

1	2	3	4	5	6	7	8	9	10	11	12	13
71	Sir Bevill Granville	O	C		ipV		OP	P	C*			W
72	Daniel Elliot	O	O	O	O			*	O			T
73	Henry Flemming	O	O	O	O		O	*	O		O	T
74	*Vacant*[2]											
75	Humphrey Courteney	O			pO		O					T
76	Jn. Morice	D			U		C		O			U
77	Chas. Ld. Cheyney	O		O	O			*				T
78	Jn. Tredenham	O	O		O		O	*	O	O	O	T
79	Seymour Tredenham	O	O	*Died*	O			P*				T
80	Sir Wm. Coryton	O	O	O	O			*	O			T
81	Fras. Gwyn	O	O	O	O	T	OP	*	O	O	O	T
	Cumberland:											
82	Sir Geo. Fletcher	C	C	C	C		O		C*			W
83	Sir Jn. Lowther	C	C		C	W	C	P	C			W
84	Wm. Howard	C	C	O	iF				C			W
85	Jas. Lowther	C	C		C				C*			W
86	Sir Chas. Gerard	O	O		O	T	O		O			T
87	Goodwin Wharton	C	C	C	C		C	P	C*			W
	Derbyshire:											
88	Wm. M. of Hartington	C	C		C				C			W
89	Sir Gilbert Clarke	O	O	O	O		O	*	O			T
90	Ld. Henry Cavendish[3]	C	C	O	iF				O			W
91	Jn. Bagnold	O	O	O	O							T
	Devonshire:											
92	Fras. Courtenay	O	O		O		O	*	O			T
93	Sam. Rolle	O	O		O		O		O	O		T
94	Edw. Seyward	C	C	C	C				C			W
95	Joseph Tily	C	C		C				C			W
96	Sir Edw. Seymour	O	O	O	O	T		*	O	O	O	T
97	Edw. Yarde	O	O		O				O			T
98	Jn. Granville	O	O	O	O			*	O	O	O	T
99	Geo. Parker	O	O		O				O			T
100	Thos. Northmore	O			pO				O	O	O	T
101	Jn. Burrington	Do	O	C	iV				C			W
102	Art. Champneys	C	C		C		C		O		O	W
103	Nic. Hooper	O	O	O	O				O	O	O	T
104	Sir Thos. Trevor	C	C		C		C	P	C			W
105	Courtenay Croker	C	C	C	C				C			W
106	Sir Wm. Drake	O	O		O	W	O		O		O	T
107	Sir Walter Yonge	C	C	C	C	W	C	P	C*			W
108	Ld. Robt. Russell	C	C	C	C	W	C	P	C*			W
109	Ld. Jas. Russell[4]	C	C	C	C	W	C		C*			W
110	Wm. Stawell	O			pO		O		O		O	T
111	Ric. Duke	C		C	C				C*			W
112	Sir Joseph Herne	D			U		O		q			U
113	Wm. Hayn	O			pO		C		O			T
114	Jn. Elwill	C	C	C	C	W		P	C			W
115	*Sir Rowland Gwynn*[5]		C	C	C	W		P	C*			W
116	Thos. Bere	C		C	C		C		C			W
117	Chas. Ld. Spencer	C		C	C				C*			W
	Dorset:											
118	Thos. Strangeways	O	O	O	O	T	O	*	O	O	O	T
119	Thos. Freke	O	O	O	O		O	*	O	O		T
120	Ant. Ld. Ashley[3]	D	C		pC				O			W
121	Sir Nat. Napier	O			pO		O		O			T

1	2	3	4	5	6	7	8	9	10	11	12	13
122	Nat. Bond	C		O	ipF			P	C			W
123	Nat. Napier	O			pO				O	O	O	T
124	Henry Henley	C	C	C	C			P	C*			W
125	Robt. Henley	C		C	C	W			C*			W
126	Maurice Ashley	D			U				O			U
127	Michael Harvey	D	O	O	O		O		O	O		T
128	Thos. Freke	C	C		C	W	C		C			W
129	Jn. Knight	C	C	C	C			P	q			W
130	Sir Stephen Evance	C	C	C	C		C	P	C			W
131	Nic. Cary	C		C	C							W
132	Edw. Nicholas	O	C		ipL	T	C	P	C*	O	O	T
133	Sir Mat. Andrews	D	C	C	C	W	O	P	C			W
134	Thos. Trenchard	D	C		pC	W			C			W
135	Thos. Erle	O	C	C	iV		C	P	C*			W
136	Wm. Culliford	D			U		C		C*			U
137	Ric. Fownes	O	O	O	O	T	O	*	O	O		T
	Durham:											
138	Sir Wm. Bowes	D	O	C	iV				O			W
139	Wm. Lambton	O	O	O	O	T	O		O	O	O	T
140	Chas. Montagu	Dc			pC				C*			W
141	Henry Liddell	D	C	C	C				C			W
	Essex:											
142	Sir Fras. Masham	C	C	C	C		C		C			W
143	Sir Chas. Barrington	O		O	O				O	O	O	T
144	Sir Jn. Morden	C		C	C	W			C			W
145	Sir Isaac Rebow	C	C	C	C	W	C	P	C*			W
146	Irby Montagu	C	C	C	C				C*			W
147	Sir Eliab Harvey	O	O	O	O		O	*	O			T
148	Sir Thos. Davall	O	O		O				O	O	O	T
149	Sir Thos. Middleton	C	C	C	C	W	C		C			W
	Gloucestershire:											
150	Thos. Stephens	D	O	C	iV				C			W
151	Sir Ralph Dutton	C	C	C	C	W	C		C			W
152	Robt. Payne	C	O		iX			*	C			T
153	Wm. Trye	O	O	O	O		O	*	O			T
154	Jn. Howe	O	O	O	O	W	O	*	O	O		T
155	Ric. Howe	O	O	O	O		O	*	O			T
156	Sir Fras. Winnington	O	O	O	O		O		O			T
157	Ric. Dowdeswell	C	C	C	C	W	C		C			W
	Herefordshire:											
158	Sir Herbert Croft	C	C	C	C		C		C			W
159	Sir Edw. Harley	O		O	O	W			O			T
160	Jas. Morgan	C		C	C				O			W
161	*Paul Foley*	*The Speaker*										
162	Thos. Ld. Coningsby	C	C	C	C		O	P	C*			W
163	Jn. Dutton Colt	C	C	C	C	W	C	P				W
164	Robt. Price	O	O	O	O		O	*	O		O	T
165	Thos. Foley	O	O	O	O		O		O	O	O	T
	Hertfordshire:											
166	Thos. Halsey	O	O	O	O				O	O	O	T
167	Sir Thos. Pope Blount	C	C	C	C	W	C					W
168	Sir Sam. Grimstone	O			pO		O		O			T
169	Geo. Churchill	O	O		O		OP	P	C		O	T
170	Sir Wm. Cowper	C	C	C	C	W	OP		C			W
171	Wm. Cowper	C	C	C	C				C			W

1	2	3	4	5	6	7	8	9	10	11	12	13
	Huntingdonshire:											
172	Heneage Montagu	C	C	C	C							W
173	Ant. Hammond	O	O	O	O			*	O	O		T
174	Jn. Pocklington	C			pC				C			W
175	Ric. Montagu	O	O		O		O					T
	Kent:											
176	Phil. Sydney	C	C	C	C				C			W
177	Sir Thos. Roberts	C	C	C	C		C		C			W
178	Sir Wm. Honywood	C		C	C	W	C	P	C			W
179	Geo. Sayer	C	C		C			P	C*			W
180	Sir Clowdsley Shovell	C	C		C			P	C			W
181	Sir Joseph Williamson	O	C	C	iV		O	P	C			W
182	Sir Jn. Banks	O	O	O	O	T	O	*	O			T
183	Sir Thos. Taylor	C	*Died*		pC	W	C					W
184	Robt. Crawford	C			pC		C	P	C			W
185	Caleb Bankes	O	O	*Died*	O	T	O	*				T
	Lancashire:											
186	Jas. Stanley	C	C	C	C		C	P	C*			W
187	Sir Ralph Assheton	C			pC				C			W
188	Sir Thos. Stanley	Do			pO				O			T
189	Thos. Molineux	C	C	C	C				C*			W
190	Thos. Preston	Do			pO		O					T
191	Roger Kirkby	C	C	C	C		C	P	C*			W
192	Legh Banks	O	O	O	O			*	O			T
193	Thos. Brotherton	O	O	O	O			*	O	O		T
194	Sir Roger Bradshaigh	O	O	O	O			*	O			T
195	Peter Shakerley	O	O	O	O		O	*	O	O	O	T
196	Chris. Lister	O		C	iV				C			W
197	Ambrose Pudsey	O		C	iV				C			W
198	Wm. Norres	C	C	C	C				C			W
199	Jasper Maudit	C	C	C	C				C			W
	Leicestershire:											
200	Jn. Verney	O		O	O			.	O	O		T
201	Geo. Ashby	C	C	C	C				C			W
202	Archdale Palmer	C	C	C	C				C			W
203	Sir Edw. Abney	C	C	C	C		C		C			W
	Lincolnshire:											
204	Geo. Vis. Castleton	O	O	O	O		O	P*	O			T
205	Sir Thos. Hussey	O	O		O		O		O			T
206	Sir Jn. Bolles	O	O	O	O		O	*	O	O	O	T
207	Wm. Monson	C	C	O	iF				C			W
208	Peregrine Bertie	Do	C	O	iL		C	P	C			T
209	Sir Wm. Yorke	C	C		C	W	C		O			W
210	Art. Moore	O			pO				O		O	T
211	Sir Edw. Ayscoghe	C	C	C	C		C	P	C*			W
212	Phil. Bertie	Do	C	O	iL		O	P	C			T
213	Chas. Bertie	O	C	O	iL	T	C	P	C	O	O	T
214	Sir Jn. Brownlowe	O			pO	TW	O					T
215	Sir Wm. Ellis	O	O	C	iV	W	O		q			W
	Middlesex:											
216	Sir Jn. Wolstenholme	C	C		C				C			W
217	Sir Jn. Bucknall	C		C	C				C			W
218	Chas. Montagu	C	C	C	C		C	P	C*			W
219	Sir Stephen Fox	D	C		pC		C	P	C			W

1	2	3	4	5	6	7	8	9	10	11	12	13
220	Sir Robt. Clayton	C	C		C	W	C	P	O			W
221	Sir Jn. Fleet	D	O		pO		O		O	O		T
222	Sir Wm. Ashhurst	C		C	C	W			C*			W
223	Thos. Papillon	C	C	C	C	W		P	C			W
	Monmouthshire:											
224	Sir Chas. Kemys	C		C	C		O		C			W
225	Thos. Morgan	C			pC		C		C			W
226	Jn. Arnold	C			pC	W	C		C			C
	Norfolk:											
227	Sir Henry Hobart	C	C	C	C	W		P	C			W
228	Sir Jacob Astley	O	O	O	O				O	O		T
229	Fras. Gardiner	O	O		O				C			T
230	Thos. Blofeld	O	O	O	O		O		O	O		T
231	Sir Jn. Turner	D	C	C	C	T	O		C			W
232	Chas. Turner	D			U				C			U
233	Geo. England	O	O	C	iV	W	C		O			W
234	Sam. Fuller	O	O	C	iV		C		O			W
235	Sir Jn. Wodehouse	O	O	O	O			*	O			T
236	Jas. Sloane	O	C	C	iV				C*			W
237	Sir Robt. Howard	C	C		C	W	C	P	C			W
238	Robt. Walpole	C	C	C	C		O		C			W
	Northamptonshire:											
239	Sir St. Andrew St. John	C	C		C		O		C			W
240	Thos. Cartwright	C	O		iX			*	O		O	T
241	Gilbert Dolben	Do	O	O	O	T	C	*	O	O	O	T
242	Wm. Brownlowe	C	C	C	C		C		C*			W
243	Sir Justinian Isham	O			pO	T	O		O	O	O	T
244	Chris. Montagu	C		C	C				C*			W
245	Chas. Egerton	C	C	C	C				C*			W
246	Henry Mordant	C	C		C		C	P	C			W
247	Thos. Andrew	C	C	C	C		C		C			W
	Northumberland:											
248	Wm. Forster	O	O	O	O	T	OP		O			T
249	Phil. Bickerstaffe	O		O	O	T	C		C			T
250	Sir Wm. Blackett	O	O		O				C*			T
251	Wm. Carr	O	O		O		C		C*			T
252	Geo. Nicholas	O	C		ipL		C	P	O			T
253	Sir Henry Belasyse	O	C	C	iV			P	C*		O	W
254	Ralph Grey	C	C	C	C				C			W
255	Sam. Ogle	C	C	C	C		C		C*			W
	Nottinghamshire:											
256	Sir Scrope Howe	C	C	C	C	W	C	P	C			W
257	Jn. White	C	C	C	C		C		C			W
258	Wm. Pierrepont	C	C		C				C			W
259	Ric. Slater	C	C	C	C		OP		C*			W
260	Jn. Thornhagh	C	C	C	C		C		C*			W
261	Ric. Taylor	C		C	C		C		C			W
262	Sir Fras. Molyneux	C	C	C	C		C		C*			W
263	Sir Geo. Markham	O	O		O				O			T
	Oxfordshire:											
264	Mountague Ld. Norreys	O	O	O	O	T	O		O			T
265	Sir Robt. Jenkinson	O	O	O	O	T	O	*	O	O	O	T
266	Sir Wm. Trumbull	O	C		iU			P*	C			U

1	2	3	4	5	6	7	8	9	10	11	12	13
267	Heneage Finch	O	O	O	O		O	*	O	O	O	T
268	Sir Edw. Norreys	C	O	O	iX		O	*	O	O	O	T
269	Thos. Rowney	O	O	O	O			*	O	O	O	T
270	Jas. Bertie	O	O	O	O			*	O	O	O	T
271	Sir Thos. Littleton	C	C	C	C	W	C	P	C			W
272	Sir Robt. Dashwood	O		O	O		O	*	O			T
	Rutlandshire:											
273	Jn. Ld. Burghley	O		O	O			*	O			T
274	Bennet Sherrard	C	C	C	C	W	C		C			W
	Shropshire:											
275	Ric. Ld. Newport	C	C		C		C		C			W
276	Edw. Kynaston	O	O	O	O	T	O	*	O			T
277	Andrew Newport	O	O	O	O	T	O	*	O			T
278	Jn. Kynaston	O	O	O	O			*	O			T
279	Sir Wm. Whitmore	O	O	O	O		O		O			T
280	Sir Edw. Acton	O	O	O	O	T	O		O	O	O	T
281	Thos. Newport	C		O	ipF				C			W
282	Chas. Baldwin	Do	C		ipV				q			W
283	Sir Wm. Forrester	C	C	C	C		C	P	C*			W
284	Geo. Weld	Do	O	O	O	T	OP	*	O			T
285	Ric. More	C	C		C							W
286	Chas. Mason	C	C	C	C				C*			W
	Somersetshire:											
287	Sir Jn. Smith	O	O	O	O			*	O			T
288	Sir Jn. Trevillian	O	O	O	O			*	O			T
289	Sir Thos. Day	C	C	C	C				C			W
290	Robt. Yate	C			pC				C			W
291	Sir Thos. Estcourt	Do			pO				O			T
292	Wm. Blathwayt	C	C	C	C			P	C*			W
293	Edw. Berkley	O	O		O	T	O	*	O			T
294	Wm. Coward	O	O	O	O			P	O		O	T
295	Edw. Clarke	C	C	C	C		C	P	C*			W
296	Jn. Speke	C	C	C	C		C		C			W
297	Nat. Palmer	O	O		O	T	O		O		O	T
298	Roger Hoar	C	C	C	C				C*			W
299	Alex. Lutterell	O			pO		OP		C*		O	T
300	Jn. Sandford	O	O	O	O	T	O	*	O			T
301	Sir Fras. Wyndham	O	O	O	O				C*			T
302	Jn. Hunt	O	O	O	O		O		O		O	T
303	Sir Thos. Travell	C	C	C	C		C		C*			W
304	Sir Chas. Carteret	O	O	O	O		O	*	O			T
	Southamptonshire:											
305	Chas. M. of Winchester	C	C		C	W	C	P	C			W
306	Ric. Norton	C		C	C		C		C*			W
307	Fred. Tillney	O	O	O	O		C		O		O	T
308	Ld. Wm. Powlett	C	C	C	C	W	C	P	C*			W
309	Sir Chas. Wyndham	C			pC		C		O			W
310	Sir Ben. Newland	O	O		O	T	O		O*			T
311	Nic. Hedger	O	C	C	iV		O		C			W
312	*Vacant*[6]											
313	Henry Holmes	C	O	O	iX			P*	O			T
314	Ant. Morgan	C	C	C	C			P	C*			W
315	Robt. Mitchell	C			pC		C		C			W
316	Robt. Holt	C			pC		C		C			W
317	Sir Henry Dutton Colt	C	C	C	C				C			W

1	2	3	4	5	6	7	8	9	10	11	12	13
318	Sir Robt. Cotton	C	C	C	C	T	OP	P	C*			W
319	Ant. Sturt	O	O		O				O	O		T
320	Jn. Venables	C		C	C				C			W
321	Jas. Worseley	D	O		pO				C			T
322	Thos. Done	O	O	O	O	T	O	P*	O			T
323	Edw. Vis. Cornbury	C	C	C	C	T	C	P	C*			W
324	Wm. Ettericke	O	O	O	O	T	O	P	C	O	O	T
325	Jn. Burrard	C		C	C		C					W
326	Thos. Dore	C	C	C	C		C	P	C*			W
327	Chris. Stokes	C	C		C		C					W
328	*Vacant*[7]											
329	Jn. Smith	C	C	C	C		C	P	C*			W
330	Sir Robt. Smyth	C			pC				C			W
	Staffordshire:											
331	Jn. Gray	O	O	O	O	T		*	O			T
332	Henry Pagett	O	O	O	O				O			T
333	Sir Michael Biddulph	C	C	C	C	W	C		C			W
334	Robt. Burdett	O	O	O	O	T		*	O			T
335	Phil. Foley	O	O	O	O	W	O		O	O		T
336	Thos. Foley	O	O	O	O				O	O	O	T
337	Jn. Lawton	C	C	C	C				C			W
338	Sir Jn. Leveson Gower	O	O	O	O			*	O	O	O	T
339	Thos. Guy	C	C	C	C				C*			W
340	Sir Henry Gough	O	O	O	O	T	O	*	O	O		T
	Suffolk:											
341	Sir Gervase Elwaies	C		C	C		C		C			W
342	Sir Sam. Barnardiston	O	O	O	O				O	O	O	T
343	Sir Jn. Barker	O	O	*Died*	O	T		*				T
344	Chas. Whitaker	C	C	C	C			P	C			W
345	Sir Robt. Rich	C	C	C	C	W	C	P	C*			W
346	Henry Heveningham	C	C		C				C*			W
347	Sir Adam Felton	C		C	C							W
348	Thos. Felton	C	C		C		C	P	C			W
349	Sir Henry Johnson	O	O		O	T			O	O	O	T
350	Wm. Johnson	O	O	O	O	T			O		O	T
351	Jn. Robinson	D			U		C		C			U
352	Sir Thos. Barnardiston	O	C	C	iV		C		O			W
353	Chas. Cornwallis	C	C		C							W
354	Thos. Davenant	C		C	C							W
355	Jn. Hervey	Dc	C	C	C				*			W
356	Sir Robt. Davers	O	O	O	O	T			O	O		T
	Surrey:											
357	Sir Ric. Onslow	C	C	O	iF	W	C	P	q			W
358	Denzil Onslow	C	C	C	C	W			C			W
359	Chas. Cox	O	O	C	iV				C*			W
360	Ant. Bowyer	C	C	C	C		C		C			W
361	Thos. Howard	C	C	C	C	W	C	P	C*			W
362	Morris Thompson	C	C		C				C*			W
363	Sir Jn. Parsons	O	O	O	O				C	O		T
364	Jn. Parsons	O	O		O			*	O			T
365	Morgan Randyll	Do		O	O				O		O	T
366	Foot Onslow	C	C	C	C	W	C	P	C			W
367	Sir Jn. Thompson	C	C	to HoL	C	W						W
368	Thos. Turgis	C			pC		C		O			W
369	Geo. Woodroffe	Do	O	O	O				O		O	T
370	Geo. Rodney Bridges	C	C	C	C		C		C			W

1	2	3	4	5	6	7	8	9	10	11	12	13
	Sussex:											
371	Sir Jn. Pelham	C		C	C	W	C	P	C			W
372	Sir Wm. Thomas	C		C	C		C		C			W
373	Ric. E. of Ranelagh	C	C		C	T	C	P	C*			W
374	Wm. Elson	O	O	O	O				O	O	O	T
375	Jn. Machell	C	C	C	C	W	C		C*			W
376	Henry Yates	C			pC				C*			W
377	Sir Wm. Morley	C	O		iX			*	O			T
378	Jn. Lewknor	C	O		iU	W	O		O		O	U
379	Sir Thos. Pelham	C	C	O	iF		C		C			W
380	Henry Pelham	C	C	C	C				C			W
381	Henry Priestman	C	C	C	C			P	C			W
382	Jn. Pery	O	O	O	O		O		O			T
383	Nic. Barbon	O	C		ipL		C		O			T
384	Wm. Stringer	O	O	O	O			*	O			T
385	Sir Jn. Fagge	C		C	C	W	C		O*			W
386	Sir Edw. Hungerford	D			U		OP		O			U
387	Sir Thos. Dyke	O	O	O	O		O	*	O			T
388	Jn. Conyers	O	O	O	O				O	O	O	T
389	Henry Ld. Walden	O	O		O				C			T
390	Edw. Dummer	C	C	C	C			P	C			W
	Warwickshire:											
391	Wm. Bromley	O	O	O	O		O	*	O	O	O	T
392	Andrew Archer	O	O	O	O		O	*	O			T
393	Geo. Bohun	D	O	O	O			*	O			T
394	Thos. Gery	O	O	O	O				O			T
395	Fras. Grevill	O	O	O	O			*	O	O	O	T
396	Wm. Ld. Digby	O	O	O	O	T	O	*	O			T
	Westmoreland:											
397	Sir Jn. Lowther	C	C	to HoL	C		C	P				W
398	Sir Ric. Sandford	C	C	C	C				C			W
399	Sir Wm. Twysden	O	O	O	O			*				T
400	Sir Chris. Musgrave	O	O	O	O	T	O	*	O	O	O	T
	Wiltshire:											
401	Sir Geo. Hungerford	C		O	ipF				O	O		W
402	Henry St. John	C			pC		C		O			W
403	Sir Thos. Mompesson	C	C	C	C	W	C		C			W
404	Thos. Hoby	C	C	C	C		C		C			W
405	Sir Jn. Hawles	C	C	C	C	W		P	C*			W
406	Jn. Gauntlett	C			pC			P	C		O	W
407	Sir Chas. Raleigh	C	C	C	C	W	C	P				W
408	Chas. Duncombe	C			pC		C	P		O		W
409	Robt. Hyde	O	O		O	T	O		O			T
410	Chas. Morley	O	O		O							T
411	Wm. Ashe[3]	C			pC		C		C			W
412	Edw. Ashe	C		C	C				C			W
413	Robt. Bertie	O	O	O	O			*	O	O	O	T
414	Ric. Lewis	O	O		O	T	O	*				T
415	Henry Blacke	C	C	C	C				C*			W
416	Geo. Hungerford	C		O	ipF							W
417	Sir Edw. Ernle	O	O	O	O				C			T
418	*Jn. Methuen: Absent in Portugal*: see below											
419	Alex. Popham	C	C	C	C		OP		C	O	O	W
420	Walter White	C		C	C				C			W
421	Craven Howard	D	C		pC				C			W
422	*Vacant*[8]											

1	2	3	4	5	6	7	8	9	10	11	12	13
423	Chas. Fox	O	C	O	iL	T	C	P	q*		O	T
424	Edmund Webb	O			pO		O	P	C			T
425	Sir Ralph Delavall	O			pO				C			T
426	Fras. Stonehouse	C		O	ipF				O			W
427	Thos. Neale	C	C	C	C		C	P	C*			W
428	Jn. Webb	C			pC				C			W
429	*Thos. Pitt: Absent in India*?: see below											
430	Wm. Harvey	O	O		O		O	*				T
431	Thos. Jacob	D		O	pO				O			T
432	Henry Pynnel	O	O	O	O			*	O	O		T
433	Wm. Daniell	O	O	O	O			*				T
434	Thos. Benet	D	O	O	O		O		O			T
	Worcestershire:											
435	Edw. Sandys	O	O	O	O				O			T
436	Thos. Foley	O		C	iV	W	O		C			W
437	Wm. Bromley	C	C	C	C	W	C		C			W
438	Sam. Swift	O	O	O	O			*	O	O	O	T
439	Edw. Harley	D		O	pO				O	O	O	T
440	Chas. Cocks	C	C	C	C				C			W
441	Sir Jas. Rushout	C	C	C	C	W	O					W
442	Henry Parker	O	O	O	O	T		*	O			T
443	Salwey Winnington	O		O	O				O	O	O	T
	Yorkshire:											
444	Sir Jn. Kay	Do			pO		O		C			T
445	Thos. Ld. Fairfax	C		C	C		C	P	C			W
446	Edw. Thompson	C			pC	W		P	C			W
447	Tobias Jenkins	C		O	ipF				O			W
448	Wm. St. Quintin	C	C	C	C				C*			W
449	Chas. Osborne	Do	C		ipL		C	P	C*			T
450	Robt. Byerley	O	O		O	T		*	O		O	T
451	Chris. Stockdale	C	C	C	C				C			W
452	Art. Vis. Irwin	C	C		C			P	C			W
453	Sir Chas. Hotham	C	C	C	C				C			W
454	Jn. Aislaby	O		C	iV				C			W
455	Jn. Jennings	O	C	C	iV		C	P	C*			W
456	Thos. Yorke	Dc		C	C				C			W
457	Sir Marmaduke Wyvill	D		O	pO			*	O			T
458	Thos. Frankland	C	C	C	C		C	P	C*			W
459	Hugh Bethell	D		C	pC				C			W
460	Thos. Harrison	O		O	O				C			T
461	Sir Henry Goodricke	C	C		C		OP	P	C			W
462	Sir Wm. Strickland	C	C	C	C	W	C		C			W
463	Wm. Palmes	C	C	C	C	W	C		C*			W
464	Sir Godfrey Copley	O		O	O				O	O	O	T
465	Ric. Staines	C		C	C		C		C			W
466	Sir Michael Wentworth	O	O		O		O	*				T
467	Chris. Tancred	O			pO	T	O	P	C			T
468	Sir Michael Warton	O	O	O	O	W	O		q		O	T
469	Ralph Warton	O		O	O				O			T
470	Sir Wm. Hustler	D			U				O*			U
471	Thos. Lascelles	C			pC		O	P				W
472	Sir Wm. Lowther	C	C	C	C				C			W
473	Robt. Monckton	C	C	O	iF				O			W
	Cinque Ports:											
474	Jn. Pulteney	C	C	C	C			P	C*			W
475	Robt. Austen jun.	C	C	C	C			P	C			W

1	2	3	4	5	6	7	8	9	10	11	12	13
476	Sir Basil Dixwell	C	C	C	C			P	C*			W
477	Jas. Chadwick	C	C	C	C	W		P				W
478	Jn. Taylor	C		C	C				C			W
479	Edw. Brent	C	C	C	C							W
480	Sir Phil. Boteler	C	C		C				C			W
481	Jacob Des Boverie	C		C	C				C			W
482	*Vacant*[9]											
483	Jn. Brewer	O	C		ipV			P	C		O	W
484	Sir Jn. Austen	C	C	C	C				C			W
485	Thos. Frewen	O	O	O	O				O			T
486	Robt. Austen sen.	C		*Died*	pC	W		P				W
487	Sam. Western	C	C		C			P	C			W
488	Wm. Campion	C	C	C	C			P	C			W
489	Wm. Lowndes	C	C		C			P	C*			W
	Wales:											
490	Ric. Vis. Bulkeley	O			pO			*	O		O	T
491	Sir Wm. Williams	O	O	O	O	W		P	O			T
492	Edw. Jones	O	O	O	O	T		*				T
493	Jeffrey Jeffreys	O	O	O	O			*	O	O	O	T
494	Jn. Vis. Lisburn	C	C		C				C			W
495	Jn. Lewis	C			pC				C			W
496	Sir Rice Rudd	O		C	iV				C*			W
497	Ric. Vaughan	O	O	O	O				O			T
498	Sir Wm. Williams	O			pO			*				T
499	Sir Robt. Owen	O			pO			*				T
500	Sir Ric. Myddleton	O	O	O	O	T		*	O		O	T
501	Edw. Brereton	O	O	O	O	T		*	O		O	T
502	Sir Jn. Conway	O	O		O			*	O		O	T
503	Sir Roger Puleston	O	C	C	iV							W
504	Bussey Mansell	C			pC	W			O			W
505	Thos. Mansell	O	O	O	O	T			O		O	T
506	Hugh Nanney	O	C		ipV				C			W
507	Edw. Vaughan	O	O	O	O				O			T
508	Price Devereux	O		O	O				O			T
509	Art. Owen	O		O	O				O			T
510	Jn. Philips	O		O	O				O*			T
511	Sir Wm. Wogan	O		O	O	T			O			T
512	Jn. Jeffreys	O	O	O	O				O	O	O	T
513	Robt. Harley	O	O	O	O				O	O	O	T
	First sat after 31 January 1696:											
14b	Wm. Cheyne el: 24. ii. 96			O	pO	T			O	O	O	T
183b	Thos. Rider el: 17. ii. 96		C	C	C				C			W
185b	Thos. King el: 31. x. 96			C	pC				C*		O	W
367b	Geo. Evelyn el: 5. xi. 96			C	pC	W			O			W
418	Jn. Methuen ret. from Portugal			C	pC		C	P	C			W
429	Thos. Pitt ret. from ? India			O	pO	W	C		O			T
486b	Sir Geo. Choute el: 2. xi. 96			C	pC				C			W

Notes:

[1]Elected to sit for no. 109 after unseating Lord James Russell on petition, 13 March 1696.

[2]The elected member was also chosen for no. 70 for which he had elected to sit.

[3]Column 4 accepts the evidence of *Reflections upon a Scandalous Libel* (1697) that no. 90 and no. 120 voted for the Court and that no. 411 was absent.

[4] Unseated on 13 March 1696, after which he sat for no. 328 for which he had also been chosen.

[5] Omitted from List 3 in error by the compiler, the name of his predecessor being included both for no. 115 and for no. 227 for which he had also been chosen and for which he had elected to sit.

[6] Col. Jn. Gibson was not seated until 1 Feb. 1696.

[7] The elected member was also chosen for no. 109 for which he had elected to sit.

[8] The elected member was also chosen for no. 87 for which he had elected to sit.

[9] The elected member was also chosen for no. 399 for which he had elected to sit.

APPENDIX B

The Voting Record of Members under Queen Anne

KEY

The List or Lists used in compiling the Appendix are indicated in this Key. Further information about these lists and about other copies of them is given by R. Walcott and E. S. de Beer in their articles in *B.I.H.R.*, xiv (1936), 25–36 and xix (1942), 65–6.

Column:

1 The number in Appendix A.

2 1696 classification, Appendix A, column 6.

3 The Lords' Amendments to the Bill extending the time for taking the Abjuration (J. Oldmixon, *The History of England* (1735), 283–4):
W = Whig, for agreeing with the Lords.
T = Tory, against agreeing with the Lords.

4 The Impeachment of Dr. Henry Sacheverell, 1710 (*A List of the Members of the House of Commons who voted the Impeachment of Dr. Sacheverell For High Crimes and Misdemeanours* (1710), and *A Collection of White and Black Lists* (1715)):
W = Whig, for the Impeachment.
T = Tory, against the Impeachment.

5 List of the Members of the 1710 Parliament (Brit. Mus., Stowe MS. 223, ff. 453–6):
W = Whig
T = Tory
D = Doubtful
also: * = Member of the October Club (A. Boyer, *The Political State of Gt. Britain*, 2nd. ed. 1718, iii, 117–22)

6 The Tack, 28 Nov. 1704 (*Somers Tracts*, xii, 474–6):
O = In favour of the Tack.
None of the lists examined contains reliable evidence for those who opposed the Tack.

7 The Election of the Speaker, 25 Oct. 1705 (Speck, *B.I.H.R.*, xxxvii (1964), 21–46):
C = For Smith.
O = For Bromley.
a = Absent.
C* = Tory for Smith.
a* = Tory absent.

8 C = supported the Court on the Regency Bill proceedings, Feb. 1706 (Walcott, *B.I.H.R.*, xiv (1936), 30–3).

9 C=supported the Bill for Naturalising Foreign Protestants, 1709 (*A List of those Members of Parliament that voted for the Passing of the Act for Naturalising French Protestants* (1710)).

10 O=supported the amendments to the South Sea Bill, 25 May 1711 (Sperling, *Hist. Jour.*, iv (1961), 193).

11 O=supported the motion for No Peace without Spain, 7 Dec. 1711 (Holmes, *B.I.H.R.*, xxxiii (1960), 233–4).

12 The French Commercial Treaty 18 June 1713 (*A Collection of White and Black Lists* (1715)):

C =In favour of the Bill.

O =Against the Bill.

13 O=opposed the expulsion of Steele, 19 March 1714 (Cobbett, *Parl. Hist.*, vi, 1282–3).

1	2	3	4	5	6	7	8	9	10	11	12	13
Whigs												
1	C	W										
3	iV	W	W			C	C	C		O	O	
5	C	W	W			C	C	C				
7	C		W			C	C	C				
8	C		W			C	C	C				
18	C	W	W	W		C	C	C		O	C	
27	C	W	W	W		C	C	C				
28	C					a						
44	C		W					C				
49	C	W	W	W		C	C	C			C	
54	C					C	C					
56	iV						C					
58	C		W	W		C	C			O		
62	C		W			C	C					
64	ipV			W		C	C					
65	C	W	W	W		C	C	C	O	O	O	
85	C								O	O		O
88	C	W				C	C					
102	C				O							
107	C		W	W			C	C				
116	C	W	W	D		C	C	C				
124	C	W		D								
129	C									O		
135	iV		W	W		C	C	C		O		O
138	iV					C						
141	C	W	W					C				
142	C		W			C	C					
145	C	W	W	W		C		C		O		O
149	C							C				
157	C	W				a	C	C				
162	C	W	W			C	C	C				
171	C	W				a						

1	2	3	4	5	6	7	8	9	10	11	12	13
Whigs—*contd.*												
174	pC		W	W		C	C	C		O	O	
179	C	W										
180	C					a	C					
183b	C			D								
184	pC				O							
185b	pC	T				C						
197	iV	W										
207	iF	W	W			C	C	C				
215	iV	W	W	W		C		C			O	
216	C					C	C					
220	C	W				C	C					
222	C		W			C	C	C				
233	iV			T						O		
245	C	W	W	W		C	C	C				
246	C		W	W		a	C	C				
253	re-classified as Tory: see below											
255	C	W				C	C	C				
258	C					O	C					
260	C	W	W			C	C	C				
262	C	W										
271	C	W				C	C					
274	C											O
275	C											O
283	C	W	W	W		C	C	C				
286	C		W			C	C	C				
290	pC	W	W			C	C	C				
292	C		W			C	C	C				
295	C	W				C						
303	C			T		C	C	C		O	O	
308	C	W	W	W		C	C	C	O	O	O	O
314	C	W	W			C	C					
315	pC	W										
317	C					C	C					
326	C	W				a	C					
329	C	W	W	W		C		C	O	O	O	
333	C	W										
337	C		W					C				
339	C	W				C	C					
341	C					C	C					
348	C	W				C	C					
357	iF	W	W	W		C				O	O	O
358	C	W	W			C	C	C		O	O	
359	iV	W	W	W		C	C	C				
370	C	W	W	W		C	C	C				
372	C					a						
379	iF	W										
390	C					C						

1	2	3	4	5	6	7	8	9	10	11	12	13
Whigs—*contd.*												
398	C			W		C	C				O	O
405	C	W	W			C						
406	pC					O						
408	pC		T			O						
411	pC									O		
412	C	W	W			C	C	C		O	O	O
418	pC					a						
419	C					a						
420	C					a						
428	re-classified as Moderate Tory: see below											
437	C					C	C					
440	C	W				C	C					
448	C	W	W	W		C	C	C	O		O	O
451	C	W	W			a	C	C				
453	C	W	W	W		C	C	C				O
454	iV		T	*		C				O	O	
456	C		W			C		C				O
458	C		W	W		C	C	C	O			
462	C	W	W	W		C	C	C				
463	C		W	W		C	C	C		O		
473	iF			W		C	C	C			C	
474	C	W	W			C	C	C				
480	C					O						
483	ipV		W			C	C	C				
489	C		W	D		C*	C	C			C	
Tories re-classified as Whigs												
31	O	W	W			C	C	C				
47	O	W	W			C	C	C				
208	iL		W	W			C					
251	O	W	W			C		C				
509	O	W	W	W				C		O		
Uncertain re-classified as Whigs												
126	U		W	W		C		C		O		
232	U	W	W			C	C	C	O	O	O	O
470	U	W	W			C	C	C				
Moderate Tories												
13	O	T	T	T		C*	C				C	
43	pO			W		C*	C					
60	O			W		C*	C					
132	ipL	T	T	T*		C*	C				C	
148	O					C*						
165	O		T	T		C	C				C	
169	O					C*	C					
194	O		W	W		C*	C				C	
210	pO	T	T	T		C*	C				C	
321	pO			T		C*	C	C			C	

1	2	3	4	5	6	7	8	9	10	11	12	13
Moderate Tories—*contd.*												
324	O		T	T		C*	C					
332	O		T			C*	C					
336	O		T	T		C*						
439	pO		T	T		C*	C				C	
505	O	T	T	T		C*						
513	O		T			C*	C					
Whig re-classified as Moderate Tory												
428	pC			T			C				C	
High Tories												
11	O	T				O						
14b	pO					O						
26	O		T	T*	O	O					O	
31	re-classified as Whig: see above											
40	O	T	T	T		O						
41	O	T	T		O	O						
47	re-classified as Whig: see above											
48	O					a*						
57	O					C						
63	O	T	T	T							C	
67	O	T	T	T	O	O					C	
69	pO				O							
73	O	T		T		O						
78	O	T										
80	O	T		T		O						
81	O	T	T		O	O					C	
93	O			T		a*						
96	O		T	T	O	O						
100	pO					O						
103	O	T	T	T		O	C				C	
106	O		T	T	O	O						
118	O	T	T	T	O	O						
123	pO	T				O					C	
137	O	T	T	T	O	O					C	
139	O			T								
143	O	T			O							
152	iX						C					
153	O	T										
154	O	T										
155	O		T	T	O	O					C	
166	O		T	T								
195	O		T	T	O	O					O	O
200	O	T				O						
208	re-classified as Whig: see above											
213	iL	T	T		O	O						
228	O			T							O	

1	2	3	4	5	6	7	8	9	10	11	12	13
High Tories—*contd.*												
230	O	T				O						
235	O			T		a*					C	
240	iX		T			O						
241	O		T			O	C					
243	pO	T	T			O						
251	re-classified as Whig: see above											
265	O	T	T	T	O	O						
267	O	T			O							
268	iX				O	O						
269	O	T	T		O	O						
270	O			T	O						O	
278	O	T		T		O						
279	O					C						
280	O	T			O							
288	O		T	T							C	
294	O				O							
297	O	T				a*						
299	pO					O						
307	O			T							C	
313	iX	T	T	T	O	O						
340	O					O						
349	O		T	T		O					C	
350	O		T	T		a*					O	
356	O	T	T	T	O	O					C	
363	O		T		O	O						
365	O	T	T								O	
369	O					a*						
374	O				O	a						
388	O		T			a*					C	
389	O					C	C					
391	O	T		T	O	O						
392	O		T									
394	O	T		T	O	O						
395	O		T	T	O	O						
400	O	T										
409	O		T	T	O	O						
413	O				O	O						
417	O		W					C				
423	iL		T	T*	O	O						
429	pO			T*						O	O	O
430	O		T	T	O	O					C	
432	O				O	O						
438	O		T	T		O					C	
442	O	T			O							
443	O			T		a*					C	
444	pO					O						
450	O	T	T		O	O					C	

1	2	3	4	5	6	7	8	9	10	11	12	13
High Tories—*contd.*												
464	O					C						
468	O		T	T							O	
490	O	T		T		O						
493	O		W			O		C				
497	O		W	T		O					O	
500	O		T	T		O						
502	O					O						
507	O		T	T	O	O						
509	re-classified as Whig: see above											
512	O					O						
Whig re-classified as High Tory												
253	iV	T		T	O	O						

APPENDIX C

The Distribution of Markings on the Council of Trade List

Column:

1 The number in Appendix A.
Marks in Black
2 Crossed out and transferred to another column; original classification:
3 Ticked: *
4 Marked with a cross: +
5 Marked with an L: L
Marks in Red
6 Crossed out: ---
7 Ampersand: @
8 Tick before the name: *
9 Tick after the name: *
10 Forward sloping check before the name: /
11 Forward sloping check after the name: /
12 Backward sloping check after the name: \
13 Dot before the name: .
14 Other:
(a) Black tick cancelled in red pencil.
(b) Christian name underlined in red.
(c) A red gibbet mark.

There are no backward sloping check marks before the name and no dots after the name. The ampersands for 112, 141, 150 and 240 are superimposed on the checks; in the case of 240 this has produced what could be mistaken for a red cross. 255 might possibly have a red check under his ampersand and the tick in front of 181 could conceivably be a check or a dot. There is a faint pencil tick in front of 273. The backward sloping check after 390 could conceivably be a dot and the dot before 113 is very faint. Finally, the ampersand against 253 might refer instead to 263.

1	2	3	4	5	6	7	8	9	10	11	12	13	14
Members Finally Classified as 'Pro'													
36		*											
54											\		(c)
122			+			@							
125			+			@							
128						@							
130						@							
131						@					\		
144						@							
151						@							

1	2	3	4	5	6	7	8	9	10	11	12	13	14
Members Finally Classified as 'Pro'—*contd.*													
152			+			@							
174		*											
180			+			@		*					
184			+			@							
209						@							
217			+			@							
224								*					
226						@							
238			+	L									
240						@				/			
246		*											
255						@							
268	*Con*				---								
285			+			@							
286										/			
290			+			@							
292			+										
306	*D*												
309			+		---								
313			+		---								
314			+										
327		*											
333	*D*												
337					---								
341											\		
346					---			*					
347		*											
370					---			*					
373			+										
390											\		
401					---			*					
406			+				*						
407		*											
408			+										
419			+										
428	*D*												
445			+				*						
447			+	L									
448				L									
461			+					*					
473			+					*					
474								*					
478					---			*					
481			+										
488		*											
494		*											

1	2	3	4	5	6	7	8	9	10	11	12	13	14
Members Finally Classified as 'D' but Classified as 'Pro' on the Calculation Sheet													
51										/			
355	*Con*												
Members Finally Classified as 'Con'													
2			+										
30					---		*						
34						@							
41		*											
47			+			@						.	
70					---							.	
97												.	
99												.	
113												.	
123												.	
135												.	
168			+				*						
181			+				*						
196												.	
206			+			@							
214								*					
215			+			@							
228			+					*					
233								*					
234								*					
235								*					
251			+			@							
252						@							
253			+			@							
266	*Pro*												
294						@							
307		*											
310						@							
311	*Pro*												
349	*D*		+										
352			+										
384	*D*							*					
389									/				
395		*											
417							*						
423	*D*												
424			+				*						
425			+										
436							*						
455				L									
464							*						
467							*						

Members Finally Classified as 'Con'—*contd.*

1	2	3	4	5	6	7	8	9	10	11	12	13	14
490		*											
496			+				*						
499		*											
503	*D*							*					
506			+		---		*						
508		*											
509		*							/				(a)

Members Finally Classified as 'D' but Classified as 'Con' on the Calculation Sheet

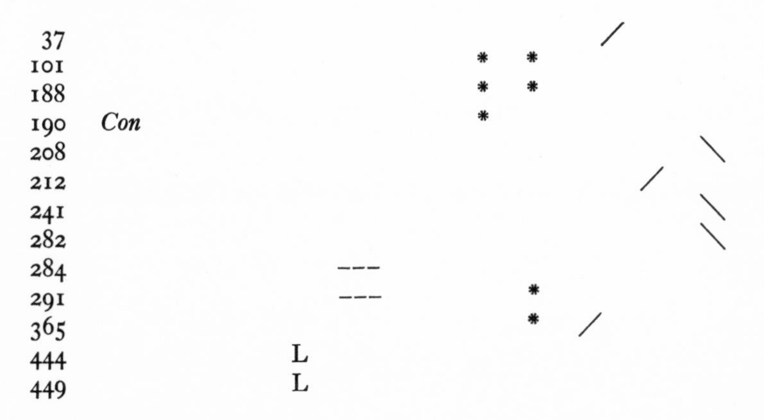

1	2	3	4	5	6	7	8	9	10	11	12	13	14
37									/				
101							*	*					
188							*	*					
190	*Con*						*						
208											\		
212										/			
241											\		
282											\		
284					---								
291					---			*					
365								*	/				
444				L									
449				L									

Members Finally Classified as 'D' but not Further Classified on the Calculation Sheet

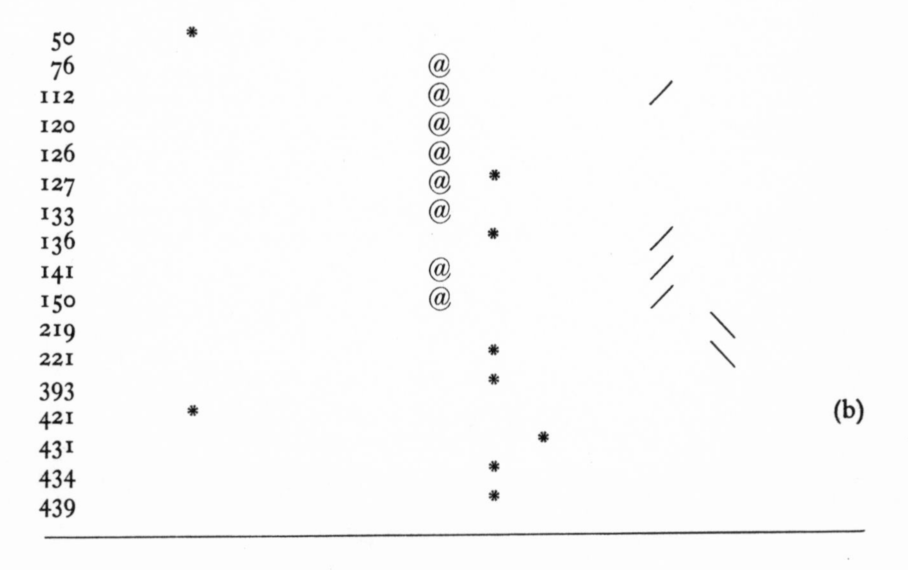

1	2	3	4	5	6	7	8	9	10	11	12	13	14
50		*											
76						@							
112						@				/			
120						@							
126						@							
127						@	*						
133						@							
136							*			/			
141						@				/			
150						@				/			
219											\		
221							*				\		
393							*						
421		*											(b)
431								*					
434							*						
439							*						

Index of Members of the House of Commons recorded in the Division Lists of 1696

Special Supplements

Nos. 1 and 2 are out of print

*No. 3 Dictionary of Writers of Thirteenth Century England J. C. RUSSELL (1936, reprinted 1967 with Additions and Corrections) £5

*No. 4 Sources for Debates of the House of Commons, 1768–1774 P. D. G. THOMAS (1959) 21s

*No. 5 Letters of Thomas Wood, Puritan, 1566–1577 P. COLLINSON (1960) 21s

†No. 6 Original Papal Documents in the Lambeth Palace Library. A Catalogue J. E. SAYERS (1967) 20s

†No. 7 Political Parties in the Reigns of William III and Anne: the Evidence of Division Lists I. F. BURTON, P. W. J. RILEY and E. ROWLANDS (1968) 20s

*Distributed by Messrs. Wm. Dawson & Sons Ltd., Back Issues Dept., Cannon House, Park Farm Road, Folkestone, Kent
†Distributed by Messrs. Constable & Co. Ltd., 10 Orange Street, London W.C.2

The Bulletin of the Institute of Historical Research is published twice a year, in May and November. The present price of each number is 15*s*. The annual subscription of 30*s*. covers two numbers and occasional Special Supplements; also the Annual Report of the Institute. The *gratis* issue of the Theses Supplement has been discontinued since 1966. The annual lists recording *Historical Research for University Degrees in the United Kingdom* now appear as a separate publication.

Forms for subscriptions or for Bankers' Orders may be obtained on application to the Secretary, Institute of Historical Research, Senate House, London W.C.1. Inquiries for back numbers of the Bulletin and the Theses Supplements should be addressed to Messrs. W. Dawson & Sons Ltd., Back Issues Department, Cannon House, Park Farm Road, Folkestone, Kent.